Development, Neoliberalism, and Islamism in South Asia

Mustahid M. Husain

Development, Neoliberalism, and Islamism in South Asia

The Case of Bangladesh

palgrave
macmillan

Mustahid M. Husain
The University of British Columbia
Kelowna, BC, Canada

ISBN 978-3-031-03108-3 ISBN 978-3-031-03113-7 (eBook)
https://doi.org/10.1007/978-3-031-03113-7

This Palgrave Macmillan imprint is published by the registered company Springer Nature Switzerland AG
The registered company address is: Gewerbestrasse 11, 6330 Cham, Switzerland

To Azaan, Aalina, and Shuchita.

Preface

Ethics approval for this research was granted by the University of British Columbia Okanagan Behavioral Research Ethics Board with certificate number H12-00262. Informal ethics approval was also granted by the community leaders and informants in the study areas of Bangladesh.

A number of sections of this monograph appeared in scholarly conferences, doctoral dissertation, and academic journals including *Student Anthropologist*, *Development Policy Review*, *Development in Practice*, *Policy Futures in Education*, *Journal of Bangladesh Studies*, and *Conflict, Security and Development*.

Kelowna, Canada — Mustahid M. Husain

Acknowledgements

I am grateful to my teachers, colleagues, and friends. Particularly, my sincere gratitude to mentors and friends including Drs. Hugo De Burgos, David Geary, Taj Hashmi, Eric Li, Joanne Taylor, and John Wagner who went above and beyond their collegial and professional responsibilities to assist me with my learning, as well as to enhance my world-view. I am also grateful to Drs. Fahim Qadir and Daromir Rudnyckyj for providing me with theoretical guidance to explain the unique and under-theorized coupling of Islam and neoliberalism. Also, special thanks to Drs. Farida Khan and Ali Riaz at the *Journal of Bangladesh Studies* and Drs. Ananya Mukherjee and Haroon Akram Lodhi at the *Canadian Journal of Development Studies* for the professional, in particular editorial exposure, direction and guidance.

To my Bangladeshi participants, I express my profound appreciation of and solidarity with your struggles, strength and sense of humour. I also thank you for your willingness to share your lives, insights and perspectives with me. I thank you for your trust in me.

Contents

List of Figures

List of Tables

CHAPTER 1

Introduction

My empirical, cross-disciplinary study in Bangladesh attempts to address a central puzzle involving the construction of inequality and poverty under an overarching transformative neoliberal framework in the country. In particular my work explores the inter-linked development initiatives and programs offered by the international development aid industry, as well as the vested interests, and Islamism in the domain of state governance. I ask why, after fifty years of development initiatives that include receiving billions of dollars' worth of aid every year (The World Bank 2018c), do so many Bangladeshis continue to be victims of poverty—unable to access the basic necessities, such as shelter, water, and sanitation, as well as remain forced to seek employment in sweatshop-like working environments in Bangladesh and beyond to make ends meet? I also wonder how the applications of neoliberal framework in Bangladesh engenders specific conditions for particular outcomes, in which "othering" and violence against local secular writers and bloggers, intellectuals and critics of "fundamentalism", gay rights activists, as well as members of ethno-religious minorities such as Hindus, Buddhists, and Christians. An alternate way to frame this study is to explore the inter-connections between economic development and politics to understand why a country that invests, for example, USD 248 million to launch its own communications and broadcasting satellite (Mahmud 2018) fails to assist approximately thirty-one

M. M. Husain, *Development, Neoliberalism, and Islamism in South Asia*, https://doi.org/10.1007/978-3-031-03113-7_1

million people (18 percent of the population) that still live below the poverty level (The World Bank 2018a).

Bangladesh has been participating in global free-trade networks for the last twenty-five year between 1991 and 2016 and maintained over six percent economic growth, which increased further in 2017 to a rate of 7.65 percent (The World Bank 2018a). Such a participation started with implementing policies of privatization and deregulation resulting in the broadening of credit and the precarisation of domestic labour. Incentives included tax cuts for businesses, some of which were foreign corporations operating in Bangladesh, e.g., Airtel BD, as well as domestic family owned corporate entities, such as *Beximco, Bashundhara*, or *Pran*. An addition to this category is one of the former chiefs of the army's family venture, *IFAD Group* that, since 2009, has rapidly expanded its presence across business sectors. According to the World Bank (2018a), Bangladesh's economic growth has contributed to reducing the number of people living below the poverty line, from 80 percent in 1972 down to 18 percent in 2017 (The World Bank 2018a). While economic growth, as measured by GDP and other signs of development such as investment in infrastructure (e.g. roads and highways), is occurring in Bangladesh, claiming rapid success in reducing poverty in the country, from 80 to 18 percent, is highly problematic. It is because, in most cases, these neoliberal policies presumed efficiency of the market and went ahead with reducing state interventions in the economy that favored the more subordinate classes. Interpreting these developments through a lens that is critical of neoliberalism as these numbers mask the chronic poverty and growing social inequality between the rich and poor and the ways in which valuable resources, spent and consumed through privatization, are being used to consolidate and maintain power by a newly emerged economic-political elite class.

Understanding the production of poverty in contemporary Bangladesh, however, is not simply a post-1971 phenomenon. The current nation-state has long been situated at the margins of power in broader historical contexts, including various colonial regimes, which have contributed to forming and reforming social classes over several centuries. Interestingly, until the late eighteenth century, Bengal was one of the richest regions in the world, contributing 12 percent of global GDP (Alam 2016, 32). Most of the revenue was generated by its vast, flat, and fertile agricultural land, the intricate textile manufacturing industries, and abundance of rivers filled with varieties of fish.

However, deindustrialization of Bengali industries during the British colonial period, particularly textiles, in favour of industries in Britain, led to the hardening of religious and class divisions in Bengal, the creation of a new bureaucratic class drawn from the Brahmin caste, and the installation of a British education system in India. These changes also paved the way for economic destruction throughout the Bengal region, mainly its eastern half, now Bangladesh. After the British colonization and the independence of India and Pakistan in 1947, the restructuring of class relations in East Pakistan (Bangladesh) during the Pakistani period (1947–1971) resulted in a vacuum in terms of who took over and ran industries, businesses, and government bureaucracy. That void led to the emergence of conscious-stricken Muslim Bengali *bhadraloks* (elites) that aspired for independence from Pakistan.

When Bangladesh became independent in 1971 it was suffering from widespread illiteracy and poverty. Since gaining independence until present, one could also argue, that Bangladesh has been ruled by one totalitarian regime after another. Rather than simply discrediting the country as a "failed state," my research looks into "globally and nationally circulating discourses of development and structural forces" (Gupta 1998, 6) to understand how "under-development" in Bangladesh is the result of the continuing colonial relationships and idioms through which state development and governance as well as development aid are reconfigured in contemporary Bangladesh and how that give rise to a cultural and social disempowerment among the impoverished.

For example, structural changes in the rural economy as a result of the "Green Revolution" and the push by Western development agencies towards industrialized commercial farming has led to growing rural–urban migration and increased poverty for many former agricultural workers seeking new opportunities in the heavily populated city centres like Dhaka (Mahmood 2017). Chronic underemployment, alongside a remarkable population increase, has further exacerbated the struggles of the poor. Present-day Bangladesh ranks as the seventh most densely populated country in the world, with approximately 170 million people and a density of $1252/km^2$ (Statistics Portal 2018). Moreover, approximately 61 percent of the population of Bangladesh is of working age (15–64 years-old), while 34 percent is under the age of 14, indicating a moderate youth bulge (Kibria 2011). According to Kibria (2011, 7), "Those who are employed in the formal labour market often work 'officially' twenty-five or more hours a week but only get paid for 10 hours." While the estimated unemployment rate is relatively low, at about five percent, the problem of underemployment prevails (Kibria 2011).

In addition to some of these economic, political, and social changes, Bangladesh is facing serious climate change related problems, such as higher concentration of arsenic in the country's natural water sources. While current development policies in Bangladesh remain unable to reduce economic and social inequality in the country, climate change brings an added layer of complexity to the question of governance. These complications make Bangladesh a promising destination for the development aid industry which treats poverty reduction as a business opportunity and has more lessons than successes in reducing poverty (Riddell 2014; Apthorpe 2011; Venugopal 2018). Despite that, the aid industry is deeply invested in climate change mitigation with aims to provide the financing required for "an orderly transition to a low carbon, resilient global economy" (The World Bank 2018b).

Such a state of precarity and underemployment has encouraged rural and young Bangladeshis to work as migrant workers in the construction sites of the Middle East and beyond (Eelens and Speckmann 1990; Md. Rahman 2012). Presently, Bangladesh is one of the top ten remittance-receiving countries in the world (The World Bank Group 2016, 19). Between 1990 and 2010, the emigration rate in Bangladesh increased by almost 750 percent (Bangladesh Census 2011), which brings Bangladesh on to the list of the top five emigration countries (The World Bank Group 2016, 29). The emerging new remittance working class and the politcally connected new elite class represent two different and contrasting social groups related to the politics of development in Bangladesh (Islam 2017; Sobhan 1984).

Since the development industry in Bangladesh is now deeply embedded in its culture and class structures, I analyze development through an examination of those class relations and how they are situated vis-à-vis the politics of development and economic globalization. To understand the genesis and persistence of these class differences, I examine a broad network of actors in my study, including small, medium, and wealthy entrepreneurs, NGO aid facilitators and development professionals, and high-ranking military officials operating in Bangladesh's private and public sectors, including commercial agriculture, the ready-made garment industry, the Ministry of Transport, and privatized higher education institutions. I was also able to engage with many individuals who were the direct and indirect targets of development within these sectors, including undergraduate students and faculty at private universities, retired academics, homemakers, media personnel, small scale farmers and landless labourers. Although aid resources are meant to assist the impoverished, my findings collected from the members of these various social groups indicate that the valuable resources are mostly spent and consumed through privatization to consolidate and maintain the status quo by a newly emerged economic-political elite class in Bangladesh.

In regards to the politcally connected new elite class in Bangladesh, I also investigate the sudden rise of these networks among the wealthy and upper middle-class in the country. According to the World Ultra Wealth Report (2018, 16), "Bangladesh has been ranked the fastest growing country with an increasing number of rich population." Yet Quadir (2015, 10) remarks that presently Bangladesh is ruled by a government that is democratically elected but that nevertheless functions as a form of "kleptocratic fascism" and that this pattern of rule is responsible for the lack of social mobility for the impoverished. Rehman Sobhan agrees and highlights a historical path of dependency towards wealth creation plagued with corruption and nepotism. He further explains that the dominant classes in Bangladesh are not an autonomous ruling class but dependent on external patronage provided through the Western aid regime (1984, 202–203).

Employing a multi-sited research project over the last seven years within rural and urban Bangladesh has helped me to understand how external international forces of development—aid, privatization, and neoliberalism—shape peoples' everyday lives and articulate with politics on the ground. Emerging from the data are two important optics for the analysis of development aid in Bangladesh: (a) analysis of power; and (b) analysis of failure. By looking at how power and failure are mutually constituted in Bangladesh, I engage a holisitc and reflexive lens to understand certain contributing factors and outcomes leading to poverty and economic inequality. In particular, how the patron-client relations function in state governance, as well as how development aid 'loan/grant' process works/or not to reduce poverty in the case of Bangladesh. What is certainly evident is that the application of neoliberalism for poverty reduction has generated less than minimal success raising the question: "does it actually work?" That question is an indication of how little we still seem to know about the impact and influence of development (Riddell 2014).

Additionally, I argue, that the only way to provide agency to the non-Western world in the broader discussion of international development is through contextualizing 'development' historically and showing how it continues to inform the present, as well as aspirations for the future. This historical analysis wedded to contemporary social lives in South Asia is instrumental to address factors over-simplified or overlooked in the contemporary narratives of development, poverty, and growth (Banerjee 2018; Cooper 2005). My study attempts to fill that gap in the context of development in Bangladesh in twenty-first century led by findings that illustrate the dual-hegemonic characteristic of the state and the development aid agencies where their mutually beneficial tendencies undermine the greater good.

1.1 Presentation of Chapters

Including the introduction and conclusion, there are seven chapters in this monograph. In Chapter 2, the brief theoretical analysis is arranged in two sections. I begin by contextualizing three historical phases that underlie and contribute to the emergence of development discourse: (a) the late eighteenth-century rise of industrial capitalism, (b) the 1944 Bretton Woods Conference and the end of WWII, and (c) the breakdown of the Bretton Woods control in early 1970s on capital movements. Following my discussion of these historical periods, I provide a very specific explanation of neoliberalism: the removal of state control on capital by Bretton Woods financial institutions that consequently weakened the capacity of a state to promote national economic growth. Broadly, these changing policies and the heightened movement of global capital across borders are frequently defined as neoliberalism (Harvey 2005; Chang 2003; Husain 2019; Reinert 2007; Venugopal 2018). The main conclusions from this chapter demonstrate that state development in Bangladesh is guided by economic structural forces linked to broader neoliberal changes that result in the construction of poverty and perpetuation of socio-economic inequality through the application of over simplistic quantifiable indicators, such as GDP. These processes also overlook the outcomes of state governance on various social groups, cultures, and countries.

In Chapter 3, I explain the power void that emerged at the end of the Pakistani colonization period which facilitated the emergence of a new Bangladeshi elite class that achieved hegemonic status through forming alliance with the Western international aid/development industry. I argue that a pattern of dual hegemony has led to greater social inequalities and ever more entrenched patterns of poverty. These changes have also inspired a greater desire for in-migration from rural to urban centers, as well as out-migration beyond the Bangladeshi national borders, especially to the Middle East.

I begin the chapter with a description of the predominant class structures in post-independent Bangladesh in conjunction with an analysis of Western development aid specifically considering how aid influences class and shapes 'economic development' in the country. Following this descriptive overview, I provide an analysis of the entanglements of development and politics in present-day Bangladesh, particularly, how neoliberal measures executed through dual hegemony perpetuate external dependency and expand socio-economic inequality in the country. Finally, I further explain inequality by unpacking the capitalist and non-capitalist factors that contribute to the production and persistence of poverty in Bangladesh.

In Chapter 4, I examine the development arguments that privatization in Bangladesh is supportive of entrepreneurial and economic freedom. As a low-middle-income country with a large and young population base, Bangladesh holds immense potential for market development and growth (The World Bank 2015). However, the establishment and function of many of these enterprises remain a topic of serious concern for generating underdevelopment for many social groups.

I highlight, for example, Bangladesh's growing dependency towards foreign import as well as an emerged pattern that favours privatised higher education system, in which encouragement and funding towards empirical research in STEM and social science disciplines are obscure, if not less than minimal. I also assess the social-reality of Bangladesh Road Transport Authority (BRTA) as a public corporation, for example, where government officers and staff at a motor vehicle registration and inspection service turn a blind eye to corruption while their appointed *Dalal* (middle-men) enforcers extort "speed up" money from citizens for basic services; and, BRTA's indifference towards quality control. I argue these practices contribute to the widening economic gap in Bangladesh by generating shifts in local social reproduction. This chapter ends with an argument that there exists a disjuncture between moral philosophy and the blind application of right-wing economic prescriptions in Bangladesh.

Moving from the outcomes premature and unplanned executions of neoliberal governance framework, in Chapter 5 I weave the connection between neoliberalism and Islam in Bangladesh and reveals specific findings that assist to understand Islam-neoliberal realm vis-à-vis: (a) how

Islam in Bangladesh has aligned with neoliberal development, and (b) why then Islamic forces attack foreigners, and "others" in the nation. My explanations draw theoretical influence from José Casanova's (1994) view that market based economic systems de-privatises religion as well as François Gauthier (2019) views that presently we are in a neoliberal situation in which otherwise inassimilable economics and religion collectively construct emerging phenomena. I also re-evaluate Karl Polanyi's (2008 [1944]) embeddedness and double movement between society and market to illustrate the important, contested strand between Islam and Bangalee (Bangladeshi) cultures. Building upon this theoretical framework, I argue that the development of a majoritarian, nationalistic discourse of Islam is an outcome of an emerged phenomenon, in which social relations and production became embedded in Islam instead of Islam being embedded in the country. I call this phenomenon the "great" transformation of Bangladesh.

Moving from my analysis of the unique coupling of Islam and neoliberalism in Bangladesh, in the following Chapter 6, I present a clear linkages of Bangladesh's military resource network through three distinct levels: (a) small and medium enterprises run independently by military units and divisions. These businesses range from gas stations to more intensive ventures; (b) public sector large enterprises—this refers to organizations like the *Sena Kalyan Shangstha* that is run under a formal public sector set-up; and (c) large-scale private sector ventures (university, five-star-hotel, among others) where some or all of the resources have been drawn from the public sector. Interestingly, despite all the limitations neoliberal Bangladesh offers, empirical finds indicate the business sectors where Bangladesh military is involves offer the most efficient and transparent business practices in the country.

At the same time, these findings re-emphasize the processes that thrive through a system of patron-client relationships that operationalizes divisions on the home front and the pattern of dual hegemony on the international front, benefiting the economic-political elite while creating greater inequitable growth and underdevelopment.

I conclude with Chapter 7, where I will first discuss the most important of my findings as they bear on the general question of why development initiatives in Bangladesh appear to fail in such profound ways over the full time period of their implementation and why they continue to fail. These include: (a) Bangladeshi's divisive and fractured middle-class; (b) the "dual-hegemony" of state and aid agencies operating in the country;

(c) Bangladesh's dependency on foreign imports; (d) the failure of the education system to prepare citizens for participation in a truly democratic state; (e) an emerging sense of Islamist nationalism; and (f) the rise of the military as a development force within the state. After describing these six key findings I will then offer a few policy recommendations, such as holding fair elections and referendums and then conclude with a discussion of the limitations of my monograph and share tentative future plans for additional research. Finally, I also acknowledge the limitations of this research project and suggest future research endeavors.

References

Alam, Shahid M. 2016. *Poverty Rom the Wealth of Nations: Integration and Polarization in the Global Economy Since 1760*. Springer Science and Business Media.

Apthorpe, Raymond. 2011. "Coda: With Alice in Aidland: A Seriously Satirical Allegory." In David Mosse (ed.), *Adventures in Aidland: The Anthropology of Professionals in International Development*. New York; Oxford: Berghahn Press.

Banerjee, Somaditya. 2018. "Bhadralok Physics and the Making of Modern Science in Colonial India." PhD thesis, University of British Columbia.

Bangladesh Census. 2011. "Population and Housing. Bangladesh Bureau of Statistics. Statistics and Informatics Division. Ministry of Planning, Government of People's Republic of Bangladesh." Modified 19 August 2011. Accessed 3 March 2013. http://www.bbs.gov.bd/PageSecureReport.aspx#.

Casanova, J. 1994. *Public Religions in the Modern World*. Chicago: University of Chicago Press.

Chang, Ha-Joon. 2003. *Kicking Away the Ladder: Development Strategy in Historical Perspective*. London: Anthem Press.

Cooper, Frederick. 2005. *Colonialism in Question: Theory, Knowledge, History*. Berkeley: University of California Press.

Eelens, Frank, and J. Speckmann. 1990. "Recruitment of Labour Migrants for the Middle East: The Sri Lankan Case." *International Migration Review* 24(2):297–322.

Gauthier, F. 2019. "The Marketisation of Religion." In *Religion, Modernity, Globalisation*. London: Routledge.

Gupta, Akhil. 1998. *Postcolonial Developments: Agriculture in the Making of Modern India*. Durham: Duke University Press.

Harvey, David. 2005. *A Brief History of Neo-Liberalism*. Oxford: Oxford University Press.

Husain, Matt Mustahid. 2019. "Who Reaps the Benefit?—Dual Hegemony and the Politics of Development in Bangladesh." PhD thesis, University of British Columbia.

Islam, Nazrul. 2017. "Middle-Class in Bangladesh." *Bangladesh e-Journal of Sociology* 14(1) January:4–15. Accessed 27 August 2018. http://www.bangladeshsociology.org/BEJS14.1.pdf.

Kibria, Nazli. 2011. "Working Hard for the Money: Bangladesh Faces Challenges of Large-Scale Labour Migration." *Migration Policy Institute*. Modified 9 August. Accessed 9 September 2015. http://www.migrationpolicy.org/article/working-hard-money-bangladesh-faces-challenges-large-scale-labor-migration.

Mahmood, Muhammad. 2017. "Income Inequality and Poverty in Bangladesh." *The Financial Express*. 25 June. https://thefinancialexpress.com.bd/views/income-inequality-and-poverty-in-bangladesh-1510415084.

Mahmud, Faisal. 2018. "Bangladesh to Join Space Age Amid Skepticism About Costs." *Nikkei Asian Review*. Accessed 22 December 2018. https://asia.nikkei.com/Economy/Bangladesh-to-join-space-age-amid-skepticism-about-costs.

Polanyi, Karl. 2008 [1944]. *The Great Transformation: The Political and Economic Origins of Our Time*. Boston: Beacon Press.

Quadir, Fahim. 2015. *Civil Society in Asia: In Search of Democracy and Development in Bangladesh*. Aldershot: Ashgate.

Rahman, Mizanur Md. 2012. "Bangladeshi Labour Migration to the Gulf States: Patterns of Recruitment and Processes." *Canadian Journal of Development Studies* 33(2):214–230.

Reinert, Erik. 2007. *How Rich Countries Got Rich and Why Poor Countries Stay Poor*. London: Constable.

Riddell, Roger. 2014. *Does Foreign Aid Really Work?* New York: Oxford University Press.

Sobhan, Rehman. 1984. *The Crisis of External Dependence: The Political Economy of Foreign Aid to Bangladesh*. London, UK; Bangladesh: Zed Press University Press.

Statistics Portal. 2018. "Population Density of Bangladesh from 2005 to 2016 (in People Per Square Kilometer)." Accessed 8 October 2018. https://www.statista.com/statistics/778381/bangladesh-population-density/.

The World Bank. 2015. "Bangladesh Projects & Programs." Accessed 9 January 2015. http://www.worldbank.org/en/country/bangladesh/projects.

———. 2016. "Migration and Remittances Recent Developments and Outlook." *Migration and Development Brief* 26. Accessed 1 September 2016. http://pubdocs.worldbank.org/en/661301460400427908/MigrationandDevelopmentBrief26.pdf.

———. 2018a. "International Debt Statistics." Accessed 12 June. https://www.indexmundi.com/facts/bangladesh/ibrd-loans-and-ida-credits.

———. 2018b. "Climate Change: Overview." Accessed 2 October 2018. http://www.worldbank.org/en/topic/climatechange/overview.

———. 2018c. "FDI." https://data.worldbank.org/indicator/BX.KLT.DINV.CD.WD?end=2016&locations=BD&start=1972&view=chart.

Venugopal, Rajesh. 2018. "Neoliberalism as Concept." *Economy and Society* 44(2):165–187.

World Ultra Wealth Report. 2018. "Rich in Bangladesh Rising Faster Than Anywhere." Accessed 9 October 2018. https://www.thedailystar.net/online/news/fastest-growing-rich-population-country-bangladesh-report-1632385.

CHAPTER 2

Development, Political Economy, and Neoliberalism

This chapter provides a conceptual and theoretical framework to my study and contextualizes some of the wider debates around neoliberalism, political economy, and development and their structural influence in creating and maintaining poverty and underdevelopment—a phenomenon that includes not only lower industrial base but also various issues such as inadequate access to public infrastructure (e.g. safe drinking water and sanitation, educational institutions, and highways), widespread poverty and corruption, and high levels of environmental pollution. I begin by reviewing the various literatures associated with the concept of development, and how it is configured through historical processes, discourse, market driven phenomenon, and policy and project prescriptions. The findings are arranged in two sections. I begin with an overview of three historical phases that have contributed to our understanding of development in the modern era. These include: (a) the late eighteenth century rise of industrial capitalism, (b) the 1944 Bretton Woods Conference and the end of WWII, and (c) the breakdown of the Bretton Woods control in early 1970s on capital movements and the subsequent rise of neoliberalism. These broader market forces illuminate the varying ways development has emerged as a modern discourse that influences countries like Bangladesh. Analyzing the reasons behind these structural

M. M. Husain, *Development, Neoliberalism, and Islamism in South Asia*,
https://doi.org/10.1007/978-3-031-03113-7_2

changes better position me to approach poverty and underdevelopment, as well as to analyze critiques on post-development and alternatives to development.

2.1 Development in Context: Historical Processes and Contested Categories

As Edelman and Haugerud write, much of the debate surrounding development in the twenty-first century focuses on whether or not:

> most societies follow the same trajectory towards greater accumulation and well-being or, alternatively, whether wealth in some places or among certain social groups is causally related to poverty in other places or among other groups. Similarly, the notion of a single development trajectory implies that history, rather than reflecting the outcomes of struggles between contending social groups — including at times very localized struggles — is simply a *deux ex machina*, in which culture and political process play no role. (Edelman and Haugerud 2005, 2)

The expanding global socio-economic gap in the early twenty-first century raises important questions about development's legacy in many parts of the world (OXFAM 2017, 2019). Conventionally, development is about achieving economic growth. However, alternative definitions of development have been proposed that emphasize access to freedom and well-being. As an alternative, "development" broadly refers to expanding the real form of freedom that people can access and enjoy by altering their economic and social arrangements to make advances in well-being, living standards, and greater life prospects (Cooper and Packard 1997; Sen 2000). In the words of Amartya Sen,

> Development requires the removal of major sources of unfreedom: poverty as well as tyranny, poor economic opportunities as well as systematic social deprivation, neglect of public facilities as well as intolerance or over activity of repressive states. Despite unprecedented increases in overall opulence, the contemporary world denies elementary freedoms to vast numbers-perhaps even the majority of people. (Sen 2000, 3–4)

According to the conventional term of development, which is also closely aligned with processes of industrialization and economic growth, is often equated with modernization and globalization by integrating countries through trade, finance, and investment. Some examples that are often cited as advances in "development" are the transformation from "traditional" agricultural economies into technology based industrial production, and the shift from subsistence-based living into capital accumulation and mass consumption. As a result, in the twentieth century, development has become "a legitimizing strategy for states, and its ambiguity lends itself to discourses of citizen entitlement, as well as state control" (Edelman and Haugerud 2005, 2). However, my focus in this study is to critique the conventional approach to development as it is unfolding in Bangladesh because the ideology becomes distorted in the hands of the development industry and state governance.

While some scholars see development as an integral part of the modernization teleos, critical scholars like Arturo Escobar (2012 [1995], 4) view "development" as an insidious and destructive myth that can be considered a failed episode of Western modernity. Influenced by Foucault's analysis of power and knowledge, Escobar treats development processes as "a destructive and self-serving discourse propagated by bureaucrats and aid professionals that permanently entraps the poor in a vicious circle of passivity and misery" (Escobar 1991, 675; Edelman and Haugerud 2005, 2). It is for these reasons Escobar relies on Marxist scholar Andre Gunder Frank, who equates development with the production of underdevelopment through rendering dependency (Frank 1967, 3). Thus, as a contested concept, in this monograph I argue that is important to understand how development has emerged as a historical and modern social construct, as well as how it has become embedded in certain state governments like Bangladesh.

2.2 The Late Eighteenth Century Rise of Industrial Capitalism

The rise of the Industrial Revolution in the late eighteenth century is often associated with the ideology of development because it was the first time Europeans made significant material progress on the world stage. There are two main precursors in this period that include the rise of capitalism, which was construed and expanded through the colonization of Asia, Africa, and Americas by a few dominant European countries (e.g. England, France, Portugal, and Spain) in the fifteenth and sixteenth centuries. The other precursor in the first stage of development was the struggle that commoner Europeans faced with monarchy, religious and class conflicts that resulted in poverty, massive unemployment, alongside rapid urbanization (Cowen and Shenton 1996, 5). In this rapidly changing social landscape the work of Scottish Philosopher and political-economist Adam Smith provides some valuable insight.

According to economic historian Skinner (1999, 5–6), in 1759 Smith published *The Theory of Moral Sentiments*, in which he acknowledged that "all people had the capacity to care about others," however, according to Smith, "people often act in their self-interest, especially in economic matters and self-seeking individuals are 'led by an invisible hand' that causes them to unintentionally act in ways that still benefited society" (Skinner 1999, 6). With that, Adam Smith coined the term "national wealth" and proposed that the "wealth of a nation" is made of both farm output, as well as manufactured goods including the labour input required to produce them. In order to increase national wealth, Smith suggested, a country needs to increase its economic production through a specialized workforce. Smith reasoned that the makers of products would exchange their goods in a money-market (free-market) with workers or producers of other products. According to Smith, the development of these free-markets this can lead to natural liberty because such a system considers everyone in a society including landowners, factory owners, and workers (Skinner 1999, 6).

Adam Smith formed his theoretical arguments about free-market by expressing reservations about mercantilist trade practices that "imposed high import duties, gave subsidies to favoured companies, and granted monopolies to powerful special interests like the East India Company" (Skinner 1999, 7–8). Smith also showcased how such preferential practices limited competition, kept prices high, and made a small class of privileged manufacturers and merchants very wealthy. Highlighting the measures of the British colonial empire such as the trade restrictions imposed on the so-called British colonies in North and South America, Smith remarked, "these restrictions benefited British special interests but [were] hurtful to the general interest of society" (Skinner 1999, 6). Finally, Smith suggested that instead of helping the rich, a government needs to leave the economy alone and let the "natural course" of free-markets and free trade emerge. The role of the state in this context is to develop a robust infrastructure to enhance the free flow of people and capital, improving social conditions by educating the country's youth, avoiding larger public debt, and setting tax rates based on an individual's earnings (Skinner 1999, 8). He also adds that a state needs strong military protections in case of invasion. By making these suggestions, Smith introduced the ideal notion of economic liberalism—*laissez faire* (to leave alone) economics.

Historically, economic liberalism went hand in hand to facilitate a reformed political conscience (philosophical liberalism) in Europe that favoured the representation of intellectuals and regular working-class people in governmental or administrative decision-making. The conceptualization and narration of a "universal history" that was expressed in larger philosophical currents from the Enlightenment, illuminating human intellect, such as Marxist and Hegelian thought (Edelman and Haugerud 2005, 6), can be seen as examples achieved by the first phase of development. These intellectual traditions remain emblematic as achievements related to development.

Overall, both economic and philosophical liberalism provided impetus for the Industrial Revolution in Europe, which in turn also helped to facilitate scientific advances. Using and building upon advancements in science and technology helped to give colonizing, Western European states burgeoning industrial capabilities to exploit raw materials collected from the rest of the world, such as cotton from India and wool from New Zealand and Australia. At the same time, the deindustrialization of the industries in India by the British colonials provided the supply of raw materials for the European markets, especially British industries (Tharoor 2015, 337). These outcomes created new markets for British products in India, and elsewhere. As a result, since the late eighteenth century Western Europe and its allies, such as the United States experienced rapid economic development and infrastructural growth (Hudelson 1999, 37).

The first historical phase of development took place in Europe through the Industrial revolution during the late eighteenth century up until the early twentieth century. A rapidly changing social landscape caused by the interconnected rise of capitalism and colonization, as well as common European resentment towards monarchy, religion and class conflicts buttressed the Industrial Revolution. The introduction of the free-market concept by Adam Smith accommodating the working people's rights and political reform strengthened the accomplishments made by the first stage of development. In the following section I explain the second phase of development.

2.3 The 1944 Bretton Woods Conference and the End of WWII

Economic expansion continued beyond the first phase of development, and after the end of WWII, particularly in the 1950s, the US emerged as the world's biggest economic power and led the economic transformation of former colonized countries (Leys 1996). Such emergence of the United States as a global super economic power defines the second phase of development, which I explain in this section.

Development in the twentieth century moved towards globalization that integrated world economies through trade, finance, and investment. It began with decolonization after the end of WWII in 1945, when most of the colonized countries in Asia, Africa and Americas emerged as newly independent states. However, the harsh impact of colonization left these countries struggling with various social-economic barriers that included high unemployment, illiteracy, and widespread poverty. Therefore, in the second phase of development, the economic transformation of the colonies of British, French, Portuguese, and other European powers that comprised 28 percent of the world's population, was increasingly problematized (Leys 1996, 5). A precursor to this development phase was the establishment of Bretton Woods financial institutions—the World Bank and the International Monetary Fund (IMF)—in 1944 that established the price of gold to develop a system of fixed currency exchange. The World Bank and IMF primarily advised and assisted the post-war European countries with loans to limit their capital movement across national border, as well as to develop national economic plans to foster growth. As a result, many European countries built mega-infrastructure, such as highways, modern seaports, irrigation schemes, and hydroelectric plants (Edelman and Haugerud 2005, 6). While the World Bank and IMF assisted the European countries, in 1949 US President Harry Truman pledged to apply US scientific and technological expertise to reduce global poverty. These ideas supporting poverty alleviation and development were strongly influenced by the works of John Maynard Keynes, the main British delegate to the Bretton Woods conference in 1944, who advocated in favour of government spending as a powerhouse of economic growth, as well as an important source to generate employment (Edelman and Haugerud 2005, 6).

Building upon his insights, a new form of economic liberalism that emerged and flourished between the 1930s and 1970s, which Peck refers to as a "social market economy" (Peck 2008, 3). Despite its structural advantages that enable a country to invest on its national economic infrastructure, as well as to control the mobility of its currency across its international border, there remain some criticisms about the development approaches taken during this period. An example of such reservation includes the measures of the Western technocrats that overlooked the causes of poverty as they approached the economic transformation of the newly independent countries ('Third World'). Instead of explaining poverty as an impact of the "self-regulating process of economic growth or social change" (Cooper and Packard 1997, 1), the developed Western countries and Bretton Woods financial institutions cast poverty and development related issues "in apolitical, ahistorical, techno-managerial terms – disguising the profound political questions at stake in common interventions in agriculture, health or education programs" (Ferguson 1994, 66). Apthorpe (2011, 210–214) agrees with Ferguson to add, "[development] is peculiarly innocent of history or subject to self-serving pseudo-history." Expanding on this statement, he also argues that 'development' "tend [*sic*] to live in an eternal present" (Apthorpe 2011, 214).

Despite all these criticisms about development being ahistorical, apolitical, and techno-managerial, the Bretton Woods institutions and their technocrats assumed the development process should fit a pre-existing design and 'encouraged' the newly independent countries to cooperate with Western aid agencies and the Bretton Woods financial institutions. These functions transformed the meaning of development between the 1930s and 1970s as structural changes made in this period led to broader global economic, political, and social changes. For example, these structural changes helped the Western countries, particularly the USA and Britain, to counter the expansion of communistic ideas in the 'Third World' developing countries sponsored by the former Soviet Union (USSR). The tensions between these two political blocks led to increasing military expenditure on both sides, as well as facilitated a new phase in politics of development, which I explain in the following section.

2.4 The Breakdown of the Bretton Woods Control in Early 1970s: Capital Movements and Beyond

A third phase of understanding the politics of development began in the 1970s when the Bretton Woods financial institutions imposed structural changes in the modern era that ultimately changed the meaning of development, especially for those countries trapped by these new arrangements. For example, the Bretton Woods financial institutions removed the control of the state on capital that consequently weakened the capacity of a state to promote national economic growth. At the same time, the United States replaced gold with the US dollar as the fixed measure of currency exchange. In order to implement these changes worldwide, the US led a series of market oriented, global policy changes through the Bretton Woods financial institutions. These changing policies and the heightened movement of global capital across borders are frequently defined as neoliberalism.

According to Venugopal (2015, 165), neoliberal economic phenomenon encompasses "two very clear and distinct periods, marked by a structural break." They include: (a) the "social market economy" influenced by Keynesianism from the 1930s and early 1970s, which I explained in the previous section—the second phase of development; and (b) since the mid-1970s until present. As a result of the structural changes made during the latter stage, particularly towards the beginning of the 1970s by the Bretton Woods financial institutions and the US, the latest form of neoliberalism emerged as a "great reversal" (Palley 2005, 20) of the economic theories of John Maynard Keynes (1936), one that values the market over the state to deal with economic and social problems (Edelman and Haugerud 2005, 7; Farmer 2003, 5).

I argue that neoliberalism, which is not just a rejuvenated version of liberalism, changed the meaning of development because it values profit above all else and treats society as subordinate to the economy. As Karl Polanyi (2008 [1944], 23–24) argues, the entire tradition of modern economic thought is based on the concept of the economy as an interlocking system of markets that automatically adjust supply and demand through the price mechanism. He points out that before economists invented the free market system, the human economy, since the dawn of time, was always embedded in society. Polanyi argues that the system of self-regulating markets has subordinated society to the "logic" of the market. As a result, the self-defined "developed" [neoliberal] world now runs society "as an adjunct to the market, where instead of the economy being embedded in social relations, social relations are embedded in the economic system" (Karl Polanyi 2008 [1944], 24).

Additionally, neoliberalism directives turned money into a stateless object, as well as facilitated the subsequent deregulation of the state power in the name of globalization that generated immense political disruptions, rising socio-economic tensions, and operationalized resistance to neoliberal policies and establishments in the developing countries. For example, between the mid-1970s and early 1980s, the World Bank led by former American military general and former CEO of Ford Corporation, Robert McNamara, changed the institutional focus from helping the European countries to assisting the non-European developing countries (Habib 2011, 559–561). During this period the World Bank and IMF started to advise and 'assist' developing countries to limit state authority and monopolies (deregulation), generate ownership of private enterprises (privatization), and outsource government responsibilities. The World Bank and IMF also made developing countries abandon domestic industries that functioned as import substitutes and increase imports through integrating a global market framework based on trade, finance, and investment (Chang 2003, 3).

Previously, some developing countries, such as Argentina, Brazil, and Mexico, among others, successfully showed signs of "progress" through increased economic development and self-sufficiency based on creating strong nationalized domestic markets and providing subsidies to important industries including agriculture, as well as by increasing taxation and sustaining protectionist trade policies. However, the changing form of development—neoliberal directives—favouring private ownership was complemented by the Central Intelligence Agency (CIA) induced coups in various parts of the Asian, African, and Latin American world. Most of these measures toppled or overthrew the democratically nationalist governments in developing countries with either authoritarian or military regimes (Chang 2003; Chossudovsky 2003; Reinert 2007).

Chang (2003) and Reinert (2007) argue that the manner through which Western countries aspired to develop the 'Third World' countries contradicts the development history of the industrialized West. For example, these authors highlight the establishment of protectionist US economic policies made by Alexander Hamilton (1755–1804), who aimed to promote strong domestic industries in order to reduce foreign imports. An outcome of that process was the establishment of USA's first central bank in 1791. Chang and Reinert argue that every major economically rich and technically advanced developed country, including the USA and England practiced economic policies that protected their national companies during the process of industrial development. Once these countries had reached a level of industrial development to compete in the global market, they adopted free market approaches (Chang 2003, 51; Reinert 2007, 22–23).

For example, whereas the World Bank and IMF continue to 'advise' developing countries to deregulate state authority, as well as to cease state sponsored/subsidized industries, the USA still subsidizes and protects varieties of American products and industries, ranging from agriculture to high-tech industries (Reinert 2007, 22–23). He also shows that the US federal government located in Washington DC spends more than USD 20 billion every year as loans and guarantees to support private US companies. However, located in the same city, institutions such as the World Bank and IMF prescribe "loan conditionalities" to "developing" countries but refrain from setting up similar practices.

Building upon that contradiction, I infer from these examples that most of the developing countries prematurely entered into the free market economy before reaching a level of industrial development at which they could successfully compete in such a market environment. Highlighting the duplicity of the neoliberal Bretton Woods institutions as led by the US, Reinert (2007, 23) humourously quotes the 1820s American maxim, "Don't do as the English tell you to do, do as the English did," as well as paraphrases that remark, "Don't do as the Americans tell you to do, do as the Americans did."

Another important factor is the military strength of the industrially developed states because having a strong military force not only offers protection but also ensures that other countries respect their commitments and relevant rules of business. Therefore, the strong military capacity of the industrially developed countries complemented the expansion of neoliberalism through the Bretton Woods institutions (Harvey 2005, 2):

> The role of the state is to create and preserve an institutional framework appropriate to such practices. The state has to guarantee, for example, the quality and integrity of money. It must also set up those military, defence, police and legal structures and functions required to secure private property

> rights and to guarantee, by force if need be, the proper functioning of markets. Furthermore, if markets do not exist (in areas such as land, water, education, health care, social security, or environmental pollution) then they must be created, by state action if necessary. But beyond these tasks the state should not venture. State interventions in markets (once created) must be kept to a bare minimum because, according to the theory, the state cannot possibly possess enough information to second-guess market signals (prices) and because powerful interest groups will inevitably distort and bias state interventions (particularly in democracies) for their own benefit. (Harvey 2005, 2)

Harvey emphasises that neoliberalism is "a theory of political economic practices" rather than a "complete" political ideology because while some advocates of neoliberalism, such as the economists Hayek and Friedman and conservative politicians including Reagan and Thatcher, endorse some aspects of political liberalism, others do not, such as autocrats Deng Xiaoping and Augusto Pinochet.

These mentioned decision-makers remain known for being connected to their respective country's national politics and holding supreme authority vis-à-vis allocating government and non-government funding to national development projects. Mostly, the direct beneficiaries of such funds are the interest groups and businesses that remain closely aligned with the values and objectives of neoliberal decision makers. For example, allocation of public funds for advertisement and education are spent through corporate outlets that are owned by and/or closely associated with government decision-makers (Quadir 2015, 10).

Overall, this pattern of rule and disbursement of public resources through an unregulated banking system, lower taxes for the wealthy, and deregulated labour industry in the name of privatization deliberately empower the market, degrade the environment, and intensify capitalism. At the same time, such a process facilitates capital accumulation by a powerful few instead of allowing public resources to trickle down to all social groups within a country (Harvey 2005; Stiglitz 2008). Consequently, such neoliberal activities make the rich and powerful wealthier, as well as increase the gap between the rich and poor. Since even basic healthcare and education services must be purchased under neoliberalism, social mobility for the underprivileged and impoverished becomes even more difficult to achieve (Harvey 2005; Quadir 2015; Stiglitz 2008).

Regardless of these long-term outcomes, since the 1980s the World Bank made development aid and loans to less developed countries conditional upon those countries meeting neoliberal policy aims. Presently, these are common practices of 'development' in most developing countries. As the 1980s ended while the size of government in developing countries shrank, various non-governmental organizations (NGOs) mushroomed to carry on the public sector work in many developing countries. These NGOs practised the guidelines provided by neoliberal directives as they received funds from Bretton Woods institutions, Western governmental sources, as well as from individuals and private foundations. As a result, along with 'development' service provisions, NGOs branched into new spheres of work, such as advocacy. According to Edelman and Haugerud (2005),

> NGOs are not necessarily more dependable and often are not as separate from state interests and personnel as the ideal type implies. Many European donor NGOs, for example, obtain most of their funding from their respective governments or the European Union, which hardly makes them "non-governmental." ...They [NGOs] provide new avenues of economic mobility for some, at times contributing to inequalities of power and wealth. (Edelman and Haugerud 2005, 27)

Despite this criticism of NGOs, these institutions and their patrons—the Bretton Woods institutions and Western donors—have brought poverty to the international stage and its relationship to development aid has become central to much academic work (Easterly 2005; Mosse 2005; Mosse and Lewis 2005). The mainstream Euro-American donors made commitments to attack poverty by setting up The Millennium Development Goals (MGDs), which once again pushed poverty alleviation to the top of the global aid agenda. However, the events that took place on September 11, 2001 affected aid mechanisms that resulted in making aid once again highly political and increasingly tied to militarization. For example, "security" has emerged as a new product for aid providers and has brought defense contractors into the development aid industry (USAID 2016; Husain 2017, 342).

Despite mainstreaming the operation of neoliberal directives in development, poverty continues to remain widespread in the twenty-first century and alternatives to development continue to be elusive. Most practitioners and analysts acknowledge that a large number of development projects end up as failures (Apthorpe 2011; Escobar 2012; Mosse 2005; Ferguson 1994; Riddell 2014; Venugopal 2018). Additionally, the vast and expanding socio-economics realities illustrate disillusionment about the agents—the World Bank and IMF, bi-lateral or multi-later aid agencies, and governments, among others—that promised to replace poverty with prosperity.

I argue that neoliberalism as a phenomenon has intensified over the past couple of decades, and has become more deeply and thoroughly embedded in the economic lives of people around the world and is central to globalization, through which peoples, corporations, and governments now interact and integrate across national boundaries. Although there are several different definitions and meanings around the concept of globalization, I argue that the pace and intensity of globalization is strengthened by the hand of neoliberalism. In fact, one could argue that neoliberalism and globalization are interlinked or mutually constitutive phenomenon. According to Peck (2010, 7), when neoliberal directives are implemented in different cultural contexts through 'globalization,' the generated outcomes become significantly different versions from what the ideal free market template predicted. Labelling such outcomes as "messy hybrids," Peck emphasizes that neoliberal directives encompass narrow perspectives—"cookie-cutter, context-blind, and politically naïve"—that operate with a limited set of instruments, such as free trade, privatization, and import substitution (Peck 2010, 7). Peck further adds that these instruments fail to understand the economic structures of developing countries. By drawing on these critical perspectives I aim to show in this monograph how the international development industry and state governance in Bangladesh are not disconnected from wider economic global changes.

2.5 International Development

Although international development preceded the rise of neoliberalism, presently, it has become a critical social construct that is re-modeled upon neoliberal directives and the outcomes of the measures of the development industry can be explained through dependency and world-systems theories. I begin this section by discussing the structures of the international aid industry. There are various types of development institutions such as bilateral and multilateral international development agencies, non-governmental organizations (NGOs), and think tanks, among others. For my research and analysis, I focus primarily on the World Bank and its working model to reduce global poverty and show its connections to neoliberalism and economic globalization.

The World Bank is a leading institution in the development aid industry. It is neither a bank nor an NGO in the ordinary sense. The World Bank is a unique partnership of two main institutions that work together with the goal of reducing global poverty and supporting development in various parts of the world (The World Bank 2017). These two institutions include the International Bank for Reconstruction and Development (IBRD) and the International Development Association (IDA). While the IBRD aims to reduce poverty in middle-income and creditworthy poorer countries, the IDA focuses exclusively on the world's poorest countries. In addition to IBRD and IDA, there are three other institutions including the International Finance Corporation (IFC), the Multilateral Investment Guarantee Agency (MIGA), and the International Centre for the Settlement of Investment Disputes (ICSID). These five agencies jointly form the World Bank Group. Each of these agencies functions as an individual corporation (World Bank 2017).

It is critical to understand how the funding cycle and inner nuances of development aid unfold in a developing space because these institutions deal with taxpayers' contributions (Fig. 2.1). Based on its business model, the World Bank does not assist individual entrepreneurs; instead, the World Bank works with the government of a developing country to reach out to local entrepreneurs through their affiliated associations and business chambers in various sectors—e.g., agri-business, readymade garment industry, heavy and light machinery—that have potential for business growth and generating additional revenues and employment. This applied business model means one needs to be in the "business" network (free-market system) to have access to the aid potential. Since impoverished countries, such as Bangladesh, lack heavy industries, top economists inside the World Bank envisage that it is possible for a developing country, such as Bangladesh to do better in the global economy if its government focuses on strengthening the capacity or skills of local small and medium enterprises (SMEs). Ideally, when such organizations grow, they hire additional semi-skilled labourers. As more SMEs develop with extensive semi-skilled labour force, the better it becomes for the future of

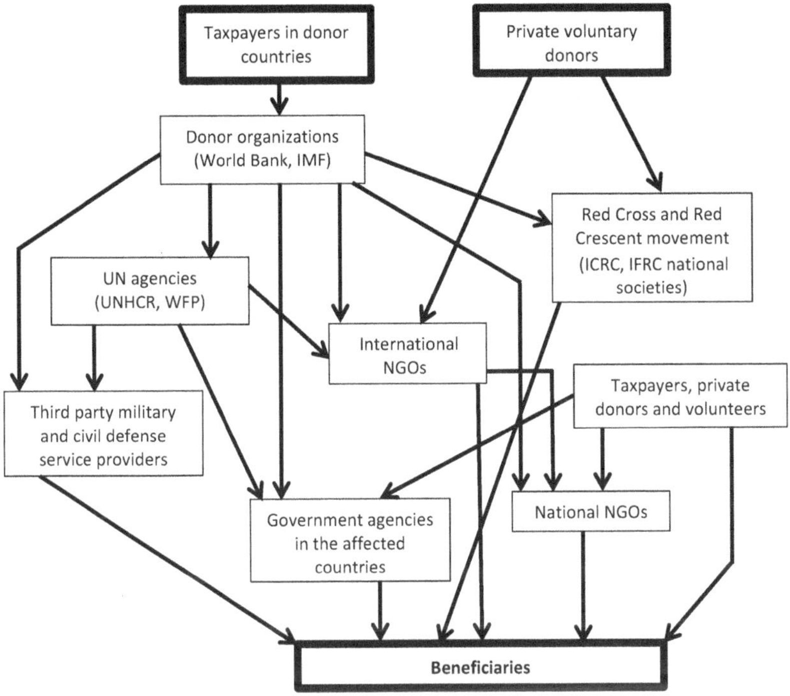

Fig. 2.1 Diagram of development aid. Based on Wood et al. (2001, 5). Permission received on 5 February 2019

economic growth and development in countries such as Bangladesh, for example.

To better allocate funding, the World Bank (2017) divides its 188-member countries and 214 economies into three categories based on per capita gross national income. These categories are the development industry's paradigms for loan or grant disbursements. These categories include:

1. Low income countries with USD 1025 or less individual per capita annual income;
2. Lower middle-income countries with USD 1026–4035 individual per capita annual income; upper middle-income economies with USD 4036–12,475; and

3. High income economies, USD 12,476 or more individual per capita annual income.

Despite its efforts to encourage global development and poverty reduction, the measures of the World Bank is often criticized due to expanding global socio-economic inequalities caused by the World Bank's failure to mitigate the challenges of democracy and redistribution (Leftwich 2005, 597–599). Urmetzer (2003, 77) analyzes the failure of the Bretton Woods financial institutions (e.g. the World Bank) and observes a dichotomy between roles played by the World Bank in promoting mixed economic tenets, as envisioned by its architect, John Keynes. Urmetzer explains, "It is somewhat hypocritical that …the World Bank to demand that Third World countries practice laissez-faire while there is so much state intervention in the First World" (Urmetzer 2003, 77). Urmetzer unpacks the World Bank's advisory and business model to argue that its practices contradict how Keynes envisioned the institution. Citing the Treaty of Versailles that enforced reparation payments of Germany by the Western Allies after the end of WWI, Urmetzer (2003, 81) remarks that as a result, Germany became overburdened with debt, which consequently provided a breeding ground for nationalism and militarism in the country. At the same time, Germany was unable to adequately engage in the international economy. Drawing a parallel to what happened in Germany after the WWI to contemporary Third World debt, Urmetzer writes that much of what is enforced by the IMF and World Bank, "is likely to produce similar outcomes" (2003, 87). Urmetzer's critiques serve as supporting arguments to how dependency creates underdevelopment.

Unlike some of the critical perspectives on the international aid industry above, Venugopal (2018, 239) takes a more balanced approach remarking that, "The constructed nature of development failure does not mean that evaluations are all fiction, that careful measurements are impossible, or that rigorous evaluations should be cast aside. It does however, [*sic*] mean that there is more to failure than failure." He shares two versions behind the failure of the development aid industry. Firstly, he cites various World Bank reports showing how the World Bank attributes the failure of development aid as "an implementation problem: that is, the failure of its borrowers (developing country governments) to implement the agreed conditionalities … in terms of a lack of ownership, weak capacity, poor governance, or political instability." Venugopal (2018, 240) also argues that instead of the borrowers, the lenders are to be blamed because most development aid projects are essentially echo narrow "cookie-cutter" visions of neoliberalism. He concludes his first observation by critiquing the development industry and remarks, aid projects remain,

> so deeply flawed that it caused negative developmental consequences, ranging variously from poverty to de-industrialisation. ... flawed structural adjustment programmes [neoliberalism] were the cause, not the consequence, of political instability and poor governance [in developing countries]. (Venugopal 2018, 240)

Secondly, Venugopal (2018, 214) explains the failure of development aid, particularly, World Bank's structural adjustment (neoliberalism) "as the product of a hidden agenda to promote the predatory economic ambition of wealthy domestic and international elites." Citing David Harvey's (2005, 64) distinction between neoliberalism in theory versus practice he argues that "the technocratic promise of a market utopia" is essentially a political project for the restoration and perpetual sustenance of capitalist class rule. Harvey's critiques support Wallerstein's (1974) original argument that world-systems encompasses both rich and poor countries and this arrangement allows rich countries extending capitalist modes of production, while impoverished countries remain supplier of cheaper human capital and markets for finished products or services, such as technology, commodity, and knowledge.

Considering the politics of development, Adam Fejerskov (2016, 366) also reveals that evaluation outcome of aid projects are essentially a "negotiated truth" because the evaluation reports generated by development aid agencies echo their own interpretation of actions and events instead of tangible connection to measurable results. Similarly, Mosse (2005, 158; 2010, 230) emphasizes on the aid industry's constructed term of 'success,' and argues that the success of a development project is influenced by particular interpretations made solely by the aid bureaucrats, as well as sustained by the other members of development industry including aid consultants.

In all, these critics argue that as a result of disseminating development assistance, aid donors and policy makers have more or less failed to learn from their past mistakes. For example, resisting realistic solutions such as lack of beneficiary driven decisions not only perpetuates the cycle of aid industry's failure but also made development further uneven by increasing the wealth gap between the developed and developing countries (Hart 2001, 650). For example, Bangladeshi critics of development aid such as Sobhan (1984, 26, 58, 146) argues that aid industry's "structural adjustment" (neoliberalism) policies did not help Bangladesh to get out of poverty; rather, they consequently put the country more in debt.

In this chapter I reviewed and discussed various historical phases around development, as well as scholarship that shed light on the international development industry such as dependency and world-systems theories. Such discussions are essential to investigate the external, international, and historical forces of development—aid, privatization, and neoliberalism—interact with internal social groups in Bangladesh. The content of this chapter sets the path to analyze the impacts of development aid and economic globalization in Bangladesh.

In the following chapter, I analyze the long and turbulent history of state-building in Bangladesh, in particular, I demonstrate that the power vacuum that emerged at the end of the Pakistani period, facilitated the emergence of a new elite class in Bangladesh that achieved hegemonic status through alliance with the international aid/development industry. That pattern of hegemony in turn creates greater inequalities and ever more entrenched patterns of poverty and migration in contemporary Bangladesh.

References

Apthorpe, Raymond. 2011. "Coda: With Alice in Aidland: A Seriously Satirical Allegory." In David Mosse (ed.), *Adventures in Aidland: The Anthropology of Professionals in International Development*. New York; Oxford: Berghahn Press.

Chang, Ha-Joon. 2003. *Kicking Away the Ladder: Development Strategy in Historical Perspective*. London: Anthem Press.

Chossudovsky, Michel. 2003. *The Globalization of Poverty and the New World Order.* Quebec: Global Research.

Cooper, Frederick, and Randall Packard. 1997. *International Development and the Social Sciences: Essays on the History and Politics of Knowledge*. Berkeley: University of California Press.

Cowen, M. P., and R. W. Shenton 1996. *Doctrines of Development*. London: Routledge.

Easterly, William. 2005. "What Did Structural Adjustment Adjust? The Association of Policies and Growth with Repeated IMF and World Bank Adjustment Loans." *Journal of Development Economics* 76(1):1–22.

Edelman, Marc, and Angelique Haugerud. 2005. *The Anthropology of Development and Globalization: From Classical Political Economy to Contemporary Neoliberalism*. Victoria: Blackwell.

Escobar, Arturo. 1991. "Anthropology and the Development Encounter: The Making and Marketing of Development Anthropology." *American Ethnologist* 18(4):658–682.

———. 2012 [1995]. *Encountering Development: The Making and Unmaking of the Third World*. Princeton, NJ: Princeton University Press.

Farmer, Paul. 2003. *Pathologies of Power Health, Human Rights, and the New War on the Poor.* Berkeley and Los Angeles: University of California Press.

Fejerskov, Adrian. 2016. "The Social Construction of Development Cooperation Success and Failure." *Forum for Development Studies* 43(3):365–383.

Ferguson, James. 1994. *The Anti-Politics Machine: "Development", Depoliticization, and Bureaucratic Power in Lesotho*. Minnesota: University of Minnesota Press.

Frank, Andre Gunder. 1967. *Capitalism and Underdevelopment in Latin America: Historical Studies of Chile and Brazil*. New York: Monthly Review Press.

Habib, Rafey. 2011. *A History of Literary Criticism: From Plato to the Present*. New York: Wiley-Blackwell.

Hart, Gillian. 2001. "Development Critiques in the 1990s: Culs de Sacs and Promising Paths." *Progress in Human Geography* 25(4):649–658.

Harvey, David. 2005. *A Brief History of Neo-Liberalism*. Oxford: Oxford University Press.

Hudelson, Richard. 1999. *Modern Political Philosophy*. New York: M.E. Sharpe.

Husain, Matt. 2017. "Aid-Effectiveness: On the Radar and Off the Radar." *Development Policy Review* 35(3):337–348.

Keynes, John Maynard. 1936. *The General Theory of Employment, Interest and Money*. London: Palgrave Macmillan.

Leftwich, Adrian. 2005. "Politics in Command: Development Studies and the Rediscovery of Social Science." *New Political Economy* 10(4):573–607.

Leys, Colin. 1996. *The Rise and Fall of Development Theory*. Oxford: Oxford Press.

Mosse, David. 2005. *Cultivating Development: An Ethnography of Aid Policy and Practice*. London: Pluto Press.

———. 2010. "A Relational Approach to Durable Poverty, Inequality and Power." *Journal of Development Studies* 46(7):1156–1178.

Mosse, David, and David Lewis (ed.). 2005. *The Aid Effect: Giving and Governing in International Development*. London: Pluto Press.

OXFAM. 2017. *An Economy for the 99%*. Canada: Oxfam. Accessed 20 January 2018. https://www.oxfam.ca/sites/default/files/file_attachments/bp-economy-for-99percent-160117-summ-embargo-en.pdf.

———. 2019. "Billionaire fortunes grew by $2.5 billion a day last year as poorest saw their wealth fall." Accessed 22 January 2019. https://www.oxfam.org/en/pressroom/pressreleases/2019-01-18/billionaire-fortunes-grew-25-billion-day-last-year-poorest-saw.

Palley, Thomas. 2005. "From Keynesianism to Neoliberalism: Shifting Paradigms." In *Neoliberalism—A Critical Reader*. London: Pluto Press.

Peck, Jamie. 2008. "Remaking Laissez Faire." *Progress in Human Geography* 32(1):3–43.

———. 2010. *Constructions of Neoliberal Reason*. Oxford: Oxford University Press.

Polanyi, Karl. 2008 [1944]. *The Great Transformation: The Political and Economic Origins of Our Time*. Boston: Beacon Press.

Quadir, Fahim. 2015. *Civil Society in Asia: In Search of Democracy and Development in Bangladesh*. Aldershot: Ashgate.

Reinert, Erik. 2007. *How Rich Countries Got Rich and Why Poor Countries Stay Poor*. London: Constable.

Riddell, Roger. 2014. *Does Foreign Aid Really Work?* New York: Oxford University Press.

Sen, Amartya. 2000. *Development as Freedom*. New York: Anchor Books.

Skinner, Andrew. 1999. *The Glasgow Edition of the Works and Correspondence of Adam Smith*. Oxford: Claredon Press.

Sobhan, Rehman. 1984. *The Crisis of External Dependence: The Political Economy of Foreign Aid to Bangladesh*. London, UK; Bangladesh: Zed Press University Press.

Stiglitz, Joseph. 2008. "Is There a Post-Washington Consensus Consensus?" In N. Serra and J. Stiglitz (eds.), *The Washington Consensus Reconsidered: Towards a New Global Governance*. Oxford: Oxford University Press.

Tharoor, Shashi. 2015. *India Shastra: Reflections on the Nation in Our Time*. Delhi: Aleph Book Company.

The World Bank. 2017. "How Do We Classify Countries?" Accessed 11 June. https://blogs.worldbank.org/opendata/new-country-classifications-income-level-2017-2018.

Urmetzer, Peter. 2003. *From Free Trade to Forced Trade: Canada in the Global Economy*. Toronto: Penguin/McGill Institute.

USAID. 2016. "Mission, Vision and Values." Accessed 12 November. https://www.usaid.gov/who-we-are/mission-vision-values.

Venugopal, Rajesh. 2015. "Neoliberalism as Concept." *Economy and Society* 44(2):165–187.

———. 2018. "Neoliberalism as Concept." *Economy and Society* 44(2):165–187.

Wallerstein, Immanuel. 1974. *The Capitalist World Economy: Essays*. New York: Cambridge University Press.

Wood, Adrian, Raymond Apthorpe, and John Borton. 2001. *Evaluating International Humanitarian Action: Reflections from Practitioners*. London: Zed Books.

CHAPTER 3

Neoliberalism, Class Structures and Politics of Development in Bangladesh

In order to illustrate Bangladesh's complex political and economic environment, this chapter focuses on the history of class relations in Bangladesh. Due to the word limitation, I skipped the long and turbulent history of state-building in Bangladesh since the Indo-Aryan period and the consequent re-shaping of class structures during the Islamic, Mughal, British, and Pakistani periods that contributed to the transformation of Bengal from one of the wealthiest regions to one of the impoverished ones. I begin the chapter with a description of the predominant class structures in post-independent Bangladesh in conjunction with an analysis of Western development aid specifically considering how aid influences class and shapes 'economic development' in the country. Following this descriptive overview, I provide an analysis of the entanglements of development and politics in present-day Bangladesh, particularly, how neoliberal measures executed through dual hegemony perpetuate external dependency and expand socio-economic inequality in the country. Finally, I further explain inequality by unpacking the capitalist and non-capitalist factors that contribute to the production and persistence of poverty in Bangladesh.

M. M. Husain, *Development, Neoliberalism, and Islamism in South Asia*, https://doi.org/10.1007/978-3-031-03113-7_3

3.1 Contemporary Bangladesh and Class Structures

Initiated by the leadership void following independence, in the past several decades Bangladesh has fallen prey to different types of totalitarian regimes, with some flavour of democracy in between. Presently, Bangladesh is ruled by a form of democratically elected government which has been described as a form of "kleptocratic fascism" (Quadir 2015, 10–11). Despite a rapid transformation towards upward economic development, for example, from USD 31 per capita GDP in 1971 up to USD 1754 per capita GDP in 2017 (The World Bank 2017a), as well as double digit economic growth for most of the 1990s fueled by the readymade garment industry, economic benefits have not "trickled down" in terms of growth, empowerment, and wealth for many of the lower and middle-classes. For example, out of the country's 170 million people, approximately, thirty-one million people (18 percent of the population) still live below the poverty level (The World Bank 2018). Although in recent years the population growth rate has slowed to 1.2 percent per year, Bangladesh remains the seventh most populous country in the world and one of the most densely populated (The World Bank 2017b). Structural changes in the rural economy caused by commercial farming have also led to increasing rural poverty and out migration to urban centers. This has consequently deepened issues of urban poverty, such as a lack of adequate housing and urban congestion (Mahmood 2017). The prevalence of child labour, rapid environmental pollution, and dangerous working conditions have only added to the downward cultural and social disempowerment of the poor in Bangladesh.

At the same time, as a result of various political, educational, and economic changes the composition and character of the middle-class has become distorted. According to Islam (2017):

> The middle-class of the 1960s was suddenly at the helm of state authority. Initially the Awami League, with one foot still in the villages, and later the military, a somewhat more Westernized group in its attitude and more urban in character, with its supporting civil bureaucracy, attained control over the economy and the polity. Through a process of nationalization and then privatization of the industries and commercial enterprises that were state owned or left behind by the West Pakistanis, a portion of the middle-class began to transform itself into a new group of "moneyed" men discarding their middle-class past. Hence, a section of this middle-class

> with access to the state power, directly or indirectly through association, acquired resources, including disinvested factories and businesses, to propel them to the "upper class" in terms of wealth and control over state power. Over the next few decades they have only consolidated their class position further and, along with a hoard of other new entrants, are on their way to crystallizing as an "Upper Class" proper. (Islam 2017, 6–7)

I argue that sections of the Bangladeshi middle-class and military class accessed the state power and transformed themselves into the "upper classes" by directly or indirectly forming alliance with the Western international aid/development industry, which prescribed the country's national development policies. According to Meghna Guhathakurta and Willem van Schendel (2013):

> When Bangladesh became independent in 1971, scholars and policymakers around the world felt that this newly independent country needed large doses of aid to survive and not only because of the colossal damage to the infrastructure that was a legacy of the Bangladesh Liberation War. Bangladesh was seen as suffering from geophysical, economic and demographic conditions that were extremely hostile to development. It was this suffering that made Bangladesh a prime challenge to the skills of development experts. (Guhathakurta and Schendel 2013, 413)

As one of the "testing laboratories" for an international donor consortium, according to Chossudovsky (2003, 159–160), since 1975 the CIA assisted the Bangladeshi military officers to overthrow the country's democratic and socialist government, and establish a more free-market economy under military patronage in the country. He also adds that the US offered substantial incentives to the Bangladeshi military government to break its traditional alliances with India and Soviet Russia by offering to train Bangladeshi economists and bureaucrats in the United States. This creation of a pool of 'Chicago Boys'—economists trained in the market driven directives of the University of Chicago—of Bangladesh helped to establish and protect the application of neoliberal directives in the country. That practice continued with an increasing flow of both US development assistance and Western foreign direct investment in Bangladesh since 1975.

Chossudovsky (2003) argues that in the mid-1980s, the military government of Bangladesh formed reservations about the growing dependency on Bretton Woods institution-based development aid. As a result, the government led by a military general attempted to cease the increasing import dependency, as well as overlooked the development advice around privatization of state-owned industries. Such a government move towards overcoming import dependency gave birth to state-sponsored projects, such as *Sho-nirbhor Bangladesh* (self-sufficient Bangladesh). The objective of these state-sponsored programs was to develop the country's industrial and communication infrastructure, as well as increase export earnings, while reducing dependency on aid and imports (Sobhan 1984, 202).

However, in retaliation to the Bangladesh Government's efforts to overcome import dependency, foreign direct investment in Bangladesh significantly plummeted in 1985 (Table 3.1). Chossudovsky (2003, 160–161) argues that the government's move towards self-sufficiency faced an abrupt response, arguably with CIA's assistance, and expressed through massive student protests that accused the military government of graft and corruption. The outcome presented Bangladesh its second democracy in 1991, which Chossudovsky labels as a "bogus democracy" because it brought compliant "political puppets" into the decision-making realm, where the Chicago Boys of Bangladesh worked with Chicago School doctrines and Washington prescriptions to formally establish and operationalize neoliberalism in Bangladesh. Such a change in

Table 3.1 Foreign direct investment inflow to Bangladesh (1972–2015)

Year	*Amount (USD)*	*Governance mandate of the government*
1972	$90,000	Democratic, Secular and Equality
1975	$1,544,000	Start of aid dependency with the a Military coup
1980	8,510,000	Military rule with moderate privatization
1985	−6,660,000	Military rulers' reservation towards aid and neoliberalism
1990	3,239,000	Inception of privatization in Bangladesh
1996	13,530,000	Pro-privatizing Right-wing governance
2000	280,385,000	Pro-privatizing Right-wing governance
2005	760,505,000	Pro-privatizing Right wing governance
2008	1,328,000,000	Military backed interim pro-privatizing Right-wing governance
2012	1,584,000,000	Pro-privatizing Right-wing governance
2013	2,603,000,000	Pro-privatizing Right-wing governance
2015	2,831,000,000	Pro-privatizing Right-wing governance

Sourced from World Bank 2018, supplemented by IMF and UN Conference on Trade and Development

Bangladesh's course of development through economic and political alterations conform to the main debate in development, as explained by dependency theory—developing societies have to follow the same trajectory towards greater accumulation and well-being prescribed by the Bretton Woods institutions (e.g. the World Bank).

In order to legitimize their enforcements, the Bretton Woods institutions celebrate various forms of success stories. For example, according to reports commissioned by the World Bank Group, rapid growth in production of low value clothing for the western market has spurred private sector growth and employment in urban Bangladeshi areas since 1991 (The World Bank 2017b). Other areas that have seen great success in light of aid assistance according to these same reports include the deregulation of agricultural markets resulting in higher production yields, as well as the diversification of employment opportunities for rural people who are long reliant on agricultural practice (Klytchnikova and Diop 2006; Sen 2003). A World Bank policy paper proclaimed that:

> The proportion of people below the poverty line has fallen sharply from close to 60 percent in 1990 to 40 percent in 2005 with a faster rate of decline since 2000. We show that the reduction in consumption poverty in Bangladesh during 2000-2005 was also mirrored by substantial improvements in living conditions–including housing characteristics, and access to sanitation facilities, electricity, and communications. (Zaman et al. 2010, 20)

Based on these claims of success by the aid donors, the Government of Bangladesh continues to receive more and more loans from Bretton Woods institutions. Particularly, according to The World Bank (2018b), in 2018 Bangladesh was one of the largest recipients of World Bank loans. Although Bangladesh Government claims the development aid industry contributes only two percent of the country's GDP (*The Daily Star* 2019), this statistic masks the fact that the country's overall banking, trading, and education industries are organized on the basis of the prescriptions of the World Bank and IMF. Based on this argument, while aid contributes only two percent of Bangladesh GDP, the majority of the formal economy is designed and structured based on the prescriptions of the Bretton Woods institutions. Presently, Bangladesh has received USD 15 billion as IBRD loans and IDA credits, but the interest rate for the loan amount remains undisclosed (Table 3.2). Interestingly,

Table 3.2 Value of Bangladesh Government's external debt (The World Bank 2018a; International Development Association IDA 2018)

Year	*(In US$)*
1971	$0.00
1972	$3,039,000
1976	$471,319,000
1981	$1,139,706,000
1986	$2,510,832,000
1991	$4,424,365,000
1996	$5,759,327,000
2001	$6,456,048,000.00
2006	$9,297,235,000.00
2011	$10,712,230,000.00
2016	$11,890,490,000.00
2017–2018	~$14,800,000,000.00

during 2017–2018 fiscal year Bangladesh received approximately USD 3 billion in loans from the World Bank (IDA 2018a). Considering the country's USD 12 billion in loans from the World Bank over the last forty-six years, it is questionable what prompted the Government of Bangladesh and the World Bank to negotiate a USD 3 billion loan while the country was preparing for a general election later in the year in December, 2018.

Presently, Bangladesh's economic elites are split into the country's two main political parties. These elites and their sub-streams of political, military and bureaucratic surrogates control the course of development in Bangladesh, as endorsed by the Bretton Woods institutions. Bangladesh's two main political parties represent two specific families, similar to the situation in West Pakistan where twenty-two families owned the majority of the industrial, banking, and insurance sectors in the unified Pakistan. Besides these elites, middle-class Bangladeshis mainly work for multinational corporations, financial institutions, garment factories and their outlets, tourism and related industry, in the arts and the media—both electronic and print, or as officials in the numerous NGOs and donor agencies (Islam 2017, 9–10). Islam notes that "the largest group who claim to be 'business men' or 'entrepreneurs' including many medium to large traders, shop owners and small-scale industrialists identify themselves as the middle-class" (Islam 2017, 10). But, unfortunately, according to Islam, the new Bangladeshi middle-class is "no longer the torch bearers of the middle-class values" (Islam 2017, 10).

He explains that since the independence of Bangladesh, "the acquisition of state power" continues to influence economic decision making. Gaining access to state power, and hence, economic resources, is also a main aspiration for many urban and rural Bangladeshis that are motivated to "change their fortunes for the better" (Islam 2017, 10). He expounds:

> With each change in government a new group of people [connected to the ruling political party] attain access to the resources of the country and they get the opportunity to change their fate. Most, if not all, of this group are fresh from the rural areas or from the lower classes but do acquire wealth in quick pace to move to the newly forming middle and upper classes. Many change their fate almost overnight and stories of "rags to riches" abound in the country. But hardly a few of these with access to the state power today are from the older middle-class, for the simple reason that the older middle-class is no longer residing in the country. (Islam 2017, 7)

Islam (2017, 10) places the Bangladeshi middle-class into three categories based on profession: (a) middle-class of professionals—physicians, engineers, lawyers, artists, and media personalities; (b) salaried middle-class—government personnel, academics, college and school teachers, executives in financial institutions, corporations, personnel in NGOs and development aid agencies, managers in factories and real estates; and (c) business middle-class—entrepreneurs, retailers, traders, shop owners, and small scale industrialists. He further subdivides Bangladeshi middle-class into upper and lower middle-classes based on "income and the accumulated wealth and assets and or access to state power, for example those of the officers in the military and the police and the elected officials of all categories because of this access to power usually command greater resources" (Islam 2017, 11).

At the same time, another sub-stream of an emerging middle-class in Bangladesh is associated with the remittance class, which holds working class jobs in foreign countries. The rise of the Bangladeshi remittance class is particularly important to understanding the changing class formations and growing inequality in the country. As of 2011, over ten million Bangladeshis lived abroad; the contract labour migration of less-skilled workers to the Arab Gulf states has been especially prominent (Ratha and Shaw 2012). Given Bangladesh's economic dependency on these labourers in the Gulf countries, from 2005 to 2015 the annual inflow of remittance increased from approximately USD 4.2 billion to nearly USD

15.31 billion in 2015 (Bangladesh Bank 2016). This makes remittance earning one of Bangladesh's largest sources of foreign revenue. Presently, Bangladesh is also one of the top five emigration countries and one of the top ten remittance-receiving countries in the world (World Bank Group 2016, 19, 29).

Islam (2017) highlights a dichotomy between the Bangladesh's remittance-sending migrant workers class versus its middle and upper classes. While the migrant workers leave their families, increasingly in the urban centers and send money home for maintaining the families, the opposite appears to be true of the Bangladeshi middle and upper classes. For example,

> The men, mostly upper class but a section of the middle-class as well, including some government officials, stay and work in Bangladesh to earn and send huge amounts of money abroad to maintain their families there. A huge community of 'Bangladeshi Begums' (wives) has recently been reported residing in Toronto, Canada to facilitate a richer and safer life for their children. (Islam 2017, 8)

It is striking that as the impoverished migrant workers remit money to Bangladesh, the upper-class Bangladeshis "drain the country of that wealth!" (Islam 2017, 8). In the following section, I explain the mutually beneficial alliance between the new Bangladeshi elite class and the Western international aid/development industry. These findings will help to interpret how the Western development paradigm contributes to the creation of an aid-bourgeois class, as well as paves the way to deepen external dependency in Bangladesh.

3.2 Dual Hegemony and Expanding Inequality

Hegemony refers to the dominance of one group or regime within a society that exerts excessive influence over other groups. In the geopolitical context, hegemony refers to the cultural dominance of one particular country over others, particularly when one state enjoys unparalleled resources and wealth that is bolstered by military power, control over natural and capital market resources, and competitive advantage to produce economies of scale (Bullock and Trombley 1999, 387–388; Dirks 2001; Schenoni 2018, 207). For example, we have seen that during the colonial era, the British established hegemony over many colonized Asian and African countries.

The Marxist theory of cultural hegemony, as coined and explicated by Antonio Gramsci (2010 [1971]), theorizes that the ruling-class is able to manipulate the value system of a society by winning the consent to its rule from those it subjugates. Cultural hegemony differs from authoritarian rule in the sense that in cultural hegemony those affected by it provide consent to the ruler (Laurie 2015, 13). Gramsci (2010 [1971]) argues that the democratic character of an intellectual individual is more important in a society than forming an intellectual class through education. Based on his idea that a capitalist state is made up of two overlapping spheres, a "political society" that rules through force and a "civil society" whose formal function represents the public consent, Gramsci interprets the role of civil society in a capitalist or bourgeois state as that sphere that upholds the concerns of the common people and the workers. However, a leadership backed by political power persuades others toward the bottom of the hierarchy chain to shape ideas and beliefs in cultural life according to the preferences of the leaders. This process involves influencing the media, universities, and religious institutions. The rulers are able to conserve their privileged positions when they can make the intellectuals accept the ideology of the dominant group. It is also possible that people who are not intellectuals, who think that they will get something out of supporting the rich and powerful, attain privileged positions. The latter situation is quite prevalent in post-colonial states, especially Bangladesh.

As Quadir (2015) explains, in Bangladesh the ruling political party is able to manipulate government agencies and bureaucracy to reward unquestionable loyalty of a subordinate employee or social group over an intellectual individual, as well as influence the country's media, universities, and religious institutions. Through enforcing such hegemony, a Bangladeshi ruling party is thus able to manipulate the value system of the country's civil society. As a result, Bangladeshi civil society becomes divisive and fragmented, as well as remains unable to represent the public consent that upholds the concerns of the common people and the workers. Quadir (2015, 10) labels such Bangladeshi practice of hegemony as "kleptocratic fascism".

Prominent Bangladeshi economist Rehman Sobhan (1984, 202) also explains how the dominant classes in Bangladesh are not an autonomous ruling class but are dependent on external patronage provided through the Western aid regime. In his words, "Whilst this class may dominate state power [sic] they in their own right are not strong enough to sustain themselves in power in the face of the mobilized masses" (Sobhan 1984, 202).

I interpret the existence and sustenance of such a Bangladeshi hegemonic dominant class by analyzing its relationship with the Western international aid/development industry. I suggest that this gives rise to what I am describing as dual hegemony, which requires both actors—the state and aid agency—jointly functional at the same time to be effective. At the same time, the absence of one makes the other inoperable and unproductive. For example, as demonstrated earlier, the Bangladesh Government accepted USD 3 billion in loans from the World Bank during the country's general election in December 2018. Considering the broader geo-political context, it would be naïve to think the US State Department did not have substantial influence on the World Bank's development policies and priorities.

Although this connection between the Bangladeshi Government and the World Bank is speculative, I will argue that it also illustrates the new Bangladeshi political elite class and the importance of retaining the elective affinity between the two through forming alliances with the international aid/development industry. At the same time, a development platform enables the World Bank to generate new revenues which the World Bank could not deliver without working with the Government of Bangladesh. In addition to preserving this nexus of dual hegemony, it also indicates how the World Bank—an external force—can continue to be in a position to influence national development policies in Bangladesh (Sunkel 1972). The example of the USD 3 billion transaction also conforms to the arguments made by Santos (1971), who foregrounds historical conditions leading to the structural inequality of the global economic system that favours some countries, particularly the United States, to the detriment of developing countries such as Bangladesh and, furthermore, it is the common people such as the working class that consequently undertake the repayment of the loans back to the Bretton Woods institutions.

In addition to the Western development aid industry, Bangladesh is also economically dependent on countries such as India, China, and Saudi Arabia. Furthermore, similarly to India, Bangladesh's economic relations to Saudi Arabia are not as linear as they are to Western countries, such as USA. Although Saudi Arabia is one of the wealthiest countries in the world due to its oil reserves, it also relies quite extensively on imported western technology to undertake resource extraction and purification of oil. Due to Saudi Arabia's technological dependency on western countries, Saudi Arabia can be described as one of the "semi-periphery" states within Wallerstein's World-Systems theory framework (Wallerstein 1976, 462). While Saudi Arabia is considered a semi-peripheral national at the global scale, I would suggest that in relation to important core countries like the USA it is ostensibly a peripheral nation but in relation to periperal states like Bangladesh it functions as a core nation.

For example, most of Bangladesh's USD 13.5 billion remittance income in 2016 was earned by workers employed at various construction sites in the Gulf Cooperation Council (GCC) countries including Saudi Arabia, Kuwait, United Arab Emirates (UAE), Bahrain, Oman, Qatar, and Yemen (World Bank 2018, Bangladesh—Country Profile). Whereas the contracting of labour employment is facilitated by the Bangladeshi economic and political elites that substantially influence the decisions made by the Government of Bangladesh, the GCC countries largely employ Bangladeshi workers due to their cheap rates. Acting as ostensibly core countries in relation to Bangladesh's peripheral status, allows GCC countires to impose external cultural and political pressure, such as in 2017 when Saudi Arabia "donated" approximately one billion dollars to construct 566 new Wahabi Islam centric mosques and madrasas. Despite the country's commitment to secularism at a constitutional level, the government is reluctant to turn down "donations" that could affect Bangladesh's labour migration to GCC countries and the remittance earnings.

Similarly, India's military, diplomatic, and humanitarian assistance during Bangladesh's war of independence in 1971 complemented India's foreign policy interests in dividing East and West Pakistan, thus transforming East Pakistan into Bangladesh (Griffiths and Hasan 2015, 233; Riaz and Bastian 2011, 153). Kabir (2006, 484) remarks, "gratitude towards India for its assistance in the war of independence [of Bangladesh] was soon replaced with a sullen resentment towards its more powerful neighbour." For example, blocking water of important rivers, particularly the Padma (Ganga in India) (Hossen 2014), and exploiting tax waivers by Indian Corporations, such as Airtel in Bangladesh (Islam 2017), keeps Bangladesh fragile in terms agricultural output, sense of a collective nationalism, revenue collection, among others.

In addition to the existing influence of India, Saudi Arabia, and the United States, China's rise as the biggest economy in the world in

2017, as well as its success in establishing the Asian Infrastructure and Investment Bank (AIIB) threatens the traditional Western dominance in development aid (AIIB 2017). In addition to the existing multiple world-systems including the United States, Western Europe, and Russia, the emergence of China as a core country complements the capitalist model of international division of labour (Wallerstein 2010, 192). This generates new wealthy classes in developing countries associated with each of these world-systems. For example, the new political and business elites in Bangladesh are the wealthy class, while the country's bureaucracy, media, universities, and other institutions in the meanwhile remain fragmented, fractured, and ineffective members of the middle-class or working class (Tasnim 2007, 179). According to Chatterjee (2004, 4), civil society in post-colonial developing countries "appears as the closed association of modern elite groups, sequestered from the wider popular life of the communities, walled up within enclaves of civic freedom and rational law." Such a non-effective, divisive state of civil society add layers of impediment to the overall wealth redistribution in the country. Complemented by historical conditions and world-systems capitalistic model, the stated internal divisions expand the economic gap between the core (e.g., the US, China) and periphery countries (e.g. Bangladesh).

Building upon these examples, as well as arguments expressed by Sunkel (1972), Santos (1971), Frank (1967), Ferraro (2008), and Wallerstein (1976), it is important to emphasize that dependency and world-systems theories help to explain the present-day Bangladeshi socio-economic-political landscape. The international influence of through development aid and free-trade (economic globalization and neoliberalism) continue to echo colonial relationships and idioms. These external forces also reconfigure the course of politics in contemporary Bangladesh that consequently gives rise to an expanding cultural and social disempowerment among the impoverished that create under-development while strengthening dual hegemony among the dominant classes (Gupta 1998, 6). In the following section, I explain the various ways through which the outcomes of underdevelopment produce poverty.

3.3 The Construction of Poverty

In this section, I analyze the capitalist and non-capitalist factors that contribute to the creation of poverty because poverty is an essential part of understanding development and the application of aid to reduce socio-economic inequality. These findings help to interpret the World Bank's poverty reduction projects in Bangladesh, as well as link the influence of capitalist world-system model (neoliberalism) to the expanding socio-economic gap in the country. These findings also suggest that poverty reduction through development is a political function with deep roots in history, despite its portrayed apolitical and ahistorical images.

According to The World Bank (2016), poverty is about not having enough resources to meet basic needs, such as food, clothing and shelter. Acknowledging that poverty is more than just not having enough money, social scientists, such as David Harvey (2005), Lakshman Yapa (1996), David Mosse (2010), and Amartya Sen (1982, 2000) provide a number of different explanations for the causes leading to poverty. For Harvey (2005), he considers capitalist and hegemonic factors, such as exploiting weak governance and high interest loans based on historical conditions as leading causes for macro-level poverty. Stiglitz (2008, 42–43) cites unregulated financial practices that operate based on the narrow objectives of free trade as another capitalist factor towards the creation of poverty. He questions the neoliberal assumption that developing countries are capable of competing in a free-market economy because it enables the development institutions, such as the World Bank to put developing countries under robust contractual obligations. As a result, when markets fail, the developing countries become obligated to pay higher interests on their loans or are subtly forced to open up their reserves and/or resources to their foreign trading partners. Also, the outcomes can make the developing countries divert funds from social projects to pay for additional financial costs. These capitalist factors directly contribute in the construction of poverty in developing countries.

Additionally, Lakshman Yapa (1996, 707) connects wealth accumulation to poverty and provides an alternative capitalist approach to the construction of poverty. Whereas free market proponents argue that we need development to reduce poverty, Yapa (1996, 707) theorizes that the process of economic development leads to a form of socially constructed scarcity that consequently creates poverty in the developing countries. He analyzes neoliberalism and argues that it picks, chooses, and revises economic assumptions, theories, and conceptualizations that benefit the "current regime of development." In his words,

> Scarcity experienced by the poor in the so-called poverty sector is manufactured outside this sector, within a nexus of relations–technical, social, ecological, cultural, political, and academic–diffused throughout the larger society. Each relation of the nexus constitutes a site at which scarcity is constructed through an interplay of discursive and non-discursive practices. The dominant discourse on development poses an obstacle to the eradication of poverty because it contributes to the creation of scarcity and conceals how those mechanisms function, thereby disempowering the poor and misleading people of goodwill. (Yapa 1996, 707)

Moving from capitalist factors to non-capitalist factors behind the construction of poverty, David Mosse (2010, 1157) argues that poverty is consistently constructed as the relation between the controllers and the controlled thereby producing inequalities. He cites the non-economic forms of social and political "exclusion" and various forms of social "categorization" such as "caste, ethnicity, and gender" that deny the impoverished access to agency and empowerment. These exclusions employ exploitations and promote unequal dependency and magnify poverty.

In the explanations provided by Nobel laureate economist Amartya Sen, he combines capitalist, non-capitalist, and hegemonic factors in his analysis of poverty. For example, he looks at the structure of ownership and entitlement relations to understand poverty in the context of famines, such as the Great Bengal Famine in 1943, the Ethiopian famines of 1973–1975 and the Bangladesh famine in 1974. In particular, he highlights the 1943 Bengal Famine arguing that the famine was not caused by a drastic shortage of available food but was due to mismanagement, corruption in food distribution channels, and price fixing (1982, 56, 79). Sen explains that the Bengal Famine deepened when British Prime Minister Churchill exploited his authority to take essential food stocks from Bengal as food reserves for British soldiers fighting on the European front during World War II (Sen 1982, 78; Tharoor 2015, 337). Although sufficient food was available in other parts of India, as explained in the previous chapter, the British administration in India, through mismanagement of the public distribution system, failed to procure and import food for the people of Bengal.

Similarly, the 1974 Bangladesh Famine, according to Sen (1982, 148–149, 161), was not caused by the destruction of the rice grain during natural disasters, such as cyclones or floods. Rather, a group of Bangladeshi traders acted in a monopolistic manner to restrict movement of grains in order to hike up demand and prices to make extra profit. The government's inability to manage the situation reinforced corruption in the distribution system, which resulted in another famine in Bangladesh. Sen compares these factors to the Irish potato famine of the nineteenth century and shows that similar human made factors contributed to the tragic outcomes in Ireland. These cases are powerful examples of the ways in which mismanagement and corruption contribute to the construction of famine and poverty.

Besides mismanagement and corruption, Amartya Sen also discusses the role of geo-politics as another factor that influences the construction of poverty. For example, since its independence in 1971, Bangladesh had been receiving regular food aid from the USA. However, this aid was tied to a clause that Bangladesh could not conduct commerce with any members of Communist countries (Sen 1982, 133–136). This put Bangladesh trade relations with Cuba and Russia at stake. In 1974, the USA threatened to cut off food aid and requested Bangladesh to cease exporting jute to Cuba. As a result, Bangladesh cancelled further jute exports to Cuba and lost valuable foreign exchange and employment within the country. The US food support arrived after the Bangladesh government complied with the US conditions, however, by this time, the local famine was largely over. Therefore, when the US supply finally arrived in Bangladesh, it played almost no role in lessening the famine. This example confirms how geo-politics can influence and facilitate Euro-American hegemony through development assistance in a developing country that undermines the urgency to reduce poverty.

Based on his overall findings on the construction of poverty and famine, Amartya Sen conclusively proves that scarcity leading to famines is caused not due to a lack of food resources but due to mismanagement and corruption within distribution systems and fixing of prices for basic necessities (Sen 1982, 56, 79, 160–166). He puts a premium on "active governance," which follows Keynesian "mixed economy,"

> Market demands are not reflections of biological needs or psychological desires, but choices based on exchange entitlement relations. If one doesn't have much to exchange, one can't demand very much, and may thus lose

> out in competition with others whose needs may be a good deal less acute, but whose entitlements are stronger. (Sen 1982, 161)

Building on this, Sen also suggests that the development industry construct a comprehensive picture of poverty and its causes before incorporating business measures to reduce poverty. He adds,

> The frequently used 'policy definition' of poverty is fundamentally flawed ... policy is a function of political organization, and depends on a variety of factors including the nature of the government, the sources of its power, and the forces exerted by other organizations. In the public policies pursued in many countries, it is in fact, hard to detect a concern with the elimination of deprivation in any obvious sense. (Sen 1982, 19, 23)

Based on all these capitalist and non-capitalist factors explained above, I theorize that poverty is a process and a product caused by the following reasons, including:

1. capitalist factors such as through the application of neoliberalism, such as imperfect market conditions—unregulated finance framework and network—leading to exploiting high interest loans and hidden fees (Harvey 2005; Stiglitz 2008, 42);
2. non-economic forms of political or social exclusion based on gender, religion, social class, and education leading to poverty and/or masking the social causes of scarcity (Mosse 2010, 1157; Yapa 1996, 707); and
3. unaccountable and non-transparent governance, such as corruption and mismanagement, as well as geo-politics (Sen 1982, 79, 148–149).

These findings indicate that the causes of poverty and poverty reduction through development aid are political functions with roots in modern history that cannot be separated from colonial relations. Therefore, I agree with Ferguson's 1994 conclusive argument on development aid that it is neither apolitical nor ahistorical, as it is often portrayed. Additionally, the manner development aid claims success in reducing poverty is problematic. According to the World Bank (2019), an individual is considered impoverished if he or she lives under US$1.90 a day, which is equivalent to BDT 161 taka. Based on such estimation, the World Bank claims presently only 18 percent of Bangladeshis live below the poverty level, whereas this number was as high as 80 percent in the past. I find such a claim incomplete because in Bangladesh, both in rural and urban areas, it is relatively easy today for an impoverished person, such as a rickshaw-puller to earn three to four hundred *taka* in a day. However, such a person still has to live with no access to pure drinking water, basic functioning sanitation, and no personal equity. In the eye of the World Bank's poverty definition, such a rickshaw-puller is not considered to be living in poverty, but I argue such a definition fails to encompass reality on the ground.

The World Bank itself acknowledges that using a multidimensional approach to calculate poverty would reveal that global poverty is "a much broader, more entrenched problem" (The World Bank 2019). They further report that the multidimensional approach to calculate poverty encompasses consumption, education, and access to basic utilities. Calculating poverty in this manner suggests it is approximately 50 percent higher than the results generated by conventional measurements practiced by the World Bank (The World Bank 2019). These arguments above provide an important opening to discuss development alternatives.

One alternative to the development aid in poverty reduction is the success attributed to Noble Laureate economist Dr. Muhammad Yunus' work and his micro-finance initiatives. He started the micro-finance program that provides small loans with low interest rates to women entrepreneurs. Yunus (2012, online) problematizes the present-day market economy (neoliberalism) to argue that the 'invisible hand' does not take care of the working class and impoverished, and is critical of the existing system because it does not deliver a new and prosperous world. Yunus argues that existing global financial structural practices are focused largely on capital accumulation, which consequently "squeezes out all kinds of social orientation out of human life and human activities" (Yunus 2012, online). Viewing this neoliberal economic system as unsustainable, Yunus asks the educated and technically savvy young Bangladeshi to step up and work with the business sector to develop a new development concept or structure that reforms neoliberalism's existing orientations.

From a different perspective anthropologist Lamia Karim (2008, 6) critiques the roles of NGOs in development because according to her analysis these institutions are actually representative of corporate capital interests (neoliberalism) in the name of empowering the impoverished, particularly women. Aiming her criticism towards Muhammad Yunus' micro-finance initiative—Grameen—she argues that,

> Grassroots globalization weakens the sovereignty of the patriarchal home family, and replaces it with the sovereignty of the market through NGOs, contracts, courts, juridical subjects, and the remaking of subjects as a community police to safeguard their investments. (Karim 2008, 6)

Interestingly, Karim overlooks critiquing Grameen's counterpart, BRAC that is considered the largest NGO in the world. I argue that BRAC functions more as a corporation than an NGO because it operates profit-driven private universities and partners with international development agencies, such as USAID, among others. While I agree with Karim (2008) that the mandate of micro-finance has a common ground with neoliberal agendas, I further support geographer Katharine Rankin's (2001, 20) research findings that indicate micro-finance mainly supports informal activities that often have low market demand. Building upon that, Khandker (2005, 2) highlights that micro-finance is more pronounced in reducing extreme rather than moderate poverty. Since 60–70 percent of Bangladeshis remain moderately poor, I argue that Bangladesh needs further alternatives to development schemes like micro-finance.

Another alternative in development is the concept of social business, which addresses social issues including gender oppression and poverty. The concept of social business was also championed by Bangladeshi economist Muhammad Yunus. It inspires corporate profit to be re-invested in the enterprise on a new social cause instead of benefitting the direct stakeholders, such as the chief executive officer (CEO), board members, and shareholders (Yunus 2010). The concept of social business has been gaining increasing worldwide popularity, particularly by drawing significant traction among various social groups that object to large CEO benefit packages and increasing corporate greed. I re-emphasize that these alternatives in development, as envisioned by Muhammad Yunus, can play a far more effective role than the existing Western dominated development industry in Bangladesh.

However, by making such statements and critiques of the current development-political nexus, Yunus has emerged as a threat to the Bangladeshi political elites, who own most of the country's economic resources and are part of the government decision making body. For example, when Muhammad Yunus announced the formation of a political party named *Nagarik Shakti* ('citizens' power') in 2007, Sheikh Hasina, chief of the Bangladesh Awami League and Bangladesh's prime minister, remarked, "sudden newcomers in politics are dangerous elements and are to be viewed with suspicion" (Reuters 2007). I argue that Yunus' arrival threatened the dual hegemony between the Bangladeshi political elites and the international development industry. For these reasons, the ruling powers politically undermined Yunus' insights on development alternatives in Bangladesh, which eventually made Yunus decide to withdraw himself from entering politics. His departure certainly satisfied the dual hegemonic alliance, which prevails while the socio-economic gap continues to expand in Bangladesh.

In the next chapter, I describe how the application of development in Bangladesh through neoliberal policies can only benefit certain privileged groups in the society. At the same time, the application of neoliberal directives in Bangladesh inevitably creates a widening wealth gap in the country, in which radical groups can exploit the impoverished. The current trajectory of development in Bangladesh can only be understood by reference to this set of relationships (e.g. dual hegemony) and their neoliberalism outcomes.

References

Asian Infrastructure and Investment Bank (AIIB). 2017. Accessed 4 August. https://www.aiib.org/en/index.html.

Bangladesh Bank. 2016. "Monthly Data of Wage Earner's Remittance." Accessed 24 August 2016. https://www.bb.org.bd/econdata/wageremitance.php.

Bullock, Alan, and Trombley, Stephen (eds.). 1999. *The New Fontana Dictionary of Modern Thought*. London: HarperCollins.

Chatterjee, Partha. 2004. *The Politics of the Governed*. New York: Columbia University Press.

Chossudovsky, Michel. 2003. *The Globalization of Poverty and the New World Order*. Quebec: Global Research.

Dirks, Nicholas. 2001. *Castes of Mind: Colonialism and the Making of Modern India*. Princeton: Princeton University Press.

Ferraro, Vincent. 2008. "Dependency Theory: An introduction." In S. Giorgio (ed.), *The Development Economics Reader*, pp. 58–64. London: Routledge.

Frank, Andre Gunder. 1967. *Capitalism and Underdevelopment in Latin America: Historical Studies of Chile and Brazil*. New York: Monthly Review Press.

Gramsci, Antonio. 2010 [1971]. *Selections from the Prison Notebooks*. In Quintin Hoare and Geoffrey Smith (eds.). New York: International Publishers.

Griffiths, Martin, and Mubashar Hasan. 2015. "Playing with Fire: Islamism and Politics in Bangladesh." *Asian Journal of Political Science* 23(2):226–241.

Guhathakurta, Meghna, and Willem van Schendel. 2013. *The Bangladesh Reader—History, Culture, Politics*. Durham and London: Duke University Press.

Gupta, Akhil. 1998. *Postcolonial Developments: Agriculture in the Making of Modern India*. Durham: Duke University Press.

Harvey, David. 2005. *A Brief History of Neo-Liberalism*. Oxford: Oxford University Press.

Hossen, Anwar. 2014. "Water Policy and Governance for the Empowerment of River Basin Communities in Rural Bangladesh." PhD thesis, University of British Columbia Okanagan.

International Development Association (IDA). 2018. "FY18 Top 10 Borrowers." Accessed 17 September 28, 2018. http://ida.worldbank.org/financing/ida-financing.

Islam, Nazrul. 2017, January. "Middle-Class in Bangladesh." *Bangladesh e-Journal of Sociology* 14(1) 4–15. Accessed 27 August 2018. http://www.bangladeshsociology.org/BEJS14.1.pdf.

Kabir, Bhuian. 2006. *Politics and Development of the Jamaat-e-Islami Bangladesh*. New Delhi: South Asian Publishers.

Karim, Lamia. 2008. "Demystifying Micro-Credit: The Grameen Bank, NGOs, and Neoliberalism in Bangladesh." *Cultural Dynamics* 20(5):5–30.

Khandker, Shahidur. 2005. *Microfinance and Poverty: Evidence Using Panel Data from Bangladesh*. Published by Oxford University Press on behalf of the World Bank.

Klytchnikova, Irina, and Ndiame Diop. 2006. "Trade Reforms, Farm Productivity, and Poverty in Bangladesh." *Policy Research Working Paper Series*, No. 3980. World Bank, Washington, DC.

Laurie, Timothy. 2015. "Masculinity Studies and the Jargon of Strategy: Hegemony, Tautology, Sense." *Journal of the Theoretical Humanities* 20(1):13–30.

Mahmood, Muhammad. 2017. "Income Inequality and Poverty in Bangladesh." *The Financial Express*. 25 June. https://thefinancialexpress.com.bd/views/income-inequality-and-poverty-in-bangladesh-1510415084.

Mosse, David. 2010. "A Relational Approach to Durable Poverty, Inequality and Power." *Journal of Development Studies* 46(7):1156–1178.

Quadir, Fahim. 2015. *Civil Society in Asia: In Search of Democracy and Development in Bangladesh*. Aldershot: Ashgate.

Rankin, Katharine. 2001. "Governing Development: Neoliberalism, Microcredit, and Rational Economic Woman." *Economy and Society* 30(1):18–37.

Ratha, Dilip, and William Shaw. 2012. "South-South Migration and Remittances." *Migration Policy Institute*. Accessed 9 September 2015. http://www.migrationpolicy.org/article/south-south-migration-and-remittances.

Reuters. 2007. "Bangladesh's Nobel Winner Names New Political Party." Accessed 14 March 2019. https://www.reuters.com/article/us-bangladesh-yunus/bangladesh-nobel-winner-names-new-political-party-idUSDHA33014220070218.

Riaz, Ali, and Jessica Bastian. 2011. "Islamist Militancy in Bangladesh: Regional and Extra-Regional Dimensions." In Ali Riaz and C. Fair (eds.), *Political Islam and Governance in Bangladesh*. London: Routledge.

Santos, Theotonio Dos. 1971. "The Structure of Dependence." *American Economic Review* 60(May 1970):231–236.

Schenoni, Luis. 2018. "The Southern African Unipolarity." *Journal of Contemporary African Studies* 36(2):207–228.

Sen, Amartya. 1982. *Poverty and Famines*. New York: Norton.

———. 2000. *Development as Freedom*. New York: Anchor Books.

Sen, Binayak. 2003. "Drivers of Escape and Descent: Changing Household Fortunes in Rural Bangladesh." *World Development* 31(3):513–534.

Sobhan, Rehman. 1984. *The Crisis of External Dependence: The Political Economy of Foreign Aid to Bangladesh*. London, UK; Bangladesh: Zed Press University Press.

Stiglitz, Joseph. 2008. "Is There a Post-Washington Consensus Consensus?" In N. Serra and J. Stiglitz (eds.), *The Washington Consensus Reconsidered: Towards a New Global Governance*. Oxford: Oxford University Press.

Sunkel, Osvaldo. 1972. "Big Business and 'Dependencia'." *Foreign Affairs* 50(April):517–531.

Tasnim, Farhat. 2007. "Civil Society in Bangladesh: Vibrant but Not Vigilant." PhD Dissertation. Department of Political Science, University of Tsukuba, Japan. Accessed 17 September 2014. http://www.tulips.tsukuba.ac.jp/limedio/dlam/B27/B2782934/1.pdf.

Tharoor, Shashi. 2015. *India Shastra: Reflections on the Nation in Our Time*. Delhi: Aleph Book Company.

The Daily Star. 2019. "Role of Foreign Aid in Bangladesh." Accessed 4 July 2019. https://www.thedailystar.net/business/role-foreign-aid-bangladesh-1603780.

The World Bank. 2016. "Migration and Remittances Recent Developments and Outlook." *Migration and Development Brief* 26. Accessed 1 September 2016. http://pubdocs.worldbank.org/en/661301460400427908/MigrationandDevelopmentBrief26.pdf.

———. 2017a. "How Do We Classify Countries?" Accessed 11 June. https://blogs.worldbank.org/opendata/new-country-classifications-income-level-2017-2018.

———. 2017b. "Bangladesh." Accessed 27 April. http://data.worldbank.org/country/bangladesh.

———. 2018a. "International Debt Statistics." Accessed 12 June. https://www.indexmundi.com/facts/bangladesh/ibrd-loans-and-ida-credits.

———. 2018b. "Lending—Bangladesh: Commitments by Fiscal Year (in millions of dollars)." Accessed 22 December 2018. http://www.worldbank.org/en/country/Bangladesh/projects.

———. 2019. "Poverty Overview." Accessed 29 June 2019. https://www.worldbank.org/en/topic/poverty/overview.

Wallerstein, Immanuel. 1976. "Semi-Peripheral Countries and the Contemporary World Crisis." *Theory and Society* 3:462–463.

Wallerstein, Immanuel. 2010. "Northeast Asia in the Multipolar World System." *Asian Perspective* 34(4):191–205.

Yapa, Lakshman. 1996. "What Causes Poverty? A Postmodern View." *Annals of the Association of American Geographers* 86(4):707–728.

Yunus, Muhammad. 2010. *Building Social Business: The New Kind of Capitalism that Serves Humanity's Most Pressing Needs*. Dhaka: University Press Limited.

———. 2012. "Insight: Ideas for Change—Social Business—Muhammad Yunus." Accessed 25 January 2019. https://www.youtube.com/watch?v=5Q2T7TEy9tE&t=4s.

Zaman, Hassan, with Ambar Narayan, and Aphichoke Kotikula. 2010. "Are Bangladesh's Recent Gains in Poverty Reduction Different from the Past?" *Bangladesh Development Studies* XXXV(1):1–26.

CHAPTER 4

Neoliberalism, Infrastructure and Philosophical Poverty

In this chapter, I discuss specific poverty reduction and development projects in Bangladesh's private and public sectors. First, I describe the impacts of a government supported move towards the privatization of institutions of higher education. Second, I describe the impact of development aid in the public sector, specifically the Bangladesh Road Transport Authority (BRTA), where government officers and staff at a motor vehicle registration and inspection service turn a blind eye to corruption while their appointed *Dalal* (middle-men) enforcers extort "speed up" money from citizens for basic services; and, BRTA's indifference towards quality control. I argue these practices contribute to the widening economic gap in Bangladesh by generating shifts in local social reproduction. My observations do not generalize to the World Bank program in totality or to all public sectors in Bangladesh where the World Bank operates. Additionally, my observations do not generalize to the measures taken by the Government of Bangladesh in managing its administration.

M. M. Husain, *Development, Neoliberalism, and Islamism in South Asia*,
https://doi.org/10.1007/978-3-031-03113-7_4

4.1 Contemporary Bangladesh, BRTA and the World Bank

As part of institutional enhancement, the World Bank offers technical assistance (TA) to various public institutions, such as the Bangladesh Road Transport Authority (BRTA), which functions as a government-run corporation. Unfortunately, "BRTA has been famous for all the wrong reasons including corruption and inefficiency," remarked Nilufar, a woman in her forties, who worked at a privately-owned company in urban Dhaka.

The public image of institutional disorder makes BRTA an ideal candidate to receive development assistance so that it can provide services to the public in a transparent and accountable manner. According to my respondent Moinul, a former development aid professional who also worked at the World Bank, "technical assistance can either be a grant or loan but the conditions of such [a] TA remain classified." Moinul added that TA funds are spent on procuring knowledge, commodities or technologies from Euro-American donor countries. For BRTA, the World Bank TA included new computers, network systems, and internet connectivity to support efficient public service (The World Bank 2003). Moinul added that "TA also covers training expenses to train the local staff, be it by an international expert or local service provider."

The disorder at BRTA, I would argue, derives from the patron-client relationship that dominates its internal networks. For example, we have seen how the local elites who constitute the political leadership in post-colonial Bangladesh are the owners of land and businesses. Political leaders, mainly business owners, tend to recruit people from their political constituencies in the rural areas, place them in their own companies and various private companies or public institutes in urban centers. BRTA is one of these. During our interview, Moinul said that the unwritten expectation of the political elites and business owner is unquestionable loyalty from employees. "The master is their *Allah* and *Bhagwan* and the world-view of these cheap laborers is shaped by the conduct of their patrons," he remarked. That settled, the political patrons in Dhaka and their surrogates in rural areas maintain a stable voter base in their respective political constituencies. Moinul's statements support my contention that class relations in Bangladesh support privatization since even government institutions such as BRTA end up being run as profit-making enterprises by business and government elites.

The stated patron-client relationship above remains an important factor in neoliberal Bangladesh (Katz 2001, 14). This patron-client relationship exploits sources of cheap labor, and the entitlement of the patron can flourish through mismanagement and corruption (Sen 1982, 299–304). In the section below, I discuss this patron-client relationship and explore the undesired social consequences heavily influencing local values, beliefs, and subjective experiences in Bangladesh.

4.2 Bangladesh Road and Transport Authority (BRTA)

BRTA has the daunting task of managing motor vehicle-related documents for approximately 2.3 million owners (BRTA). "Every day a few hundred new motor vehicles are registered in our office," remarked a BRTA official, whom I will call Sohel. According to *The Financial Express* (2014), out of 2.3 million vehicle owners registered in 2013, only 1.43 million owners held a properly issued driving license. The report's investigator indicated that fake licenses were issued by BRTA officials and the large volume of falsified driving papers known to exist further indicates the depth of corruption at BRTA.

In order to regulate driver licenses and motor vehicle document processing at BRTA, in 2003 the World Bank contributed USD 7 million to assist the Ministry of Communication in Bangladesh to construct websites where policy documents, application forms, and relevant information would be accessible to the public (The World Bank 2003). In addition, the World Bank provided BRTA with the suggested number of new computers installed with software programs, and facilitated training sessions for its staff to build necessary technical capacity (The World Bank 2003). However, the well-intentioned partnership between WB and the Bangladesh Government was undermined by the on-the-ground reality at BRTA.

BRTA is located in the Mirpur area of urban Dhaka. Its premises and vehicle testing space include a large area, approximately half a square kilometer, which holds three main administrative buildings, several makeshift offices—small areas cordoned off from one another by little more than a sheet hung over a string with a table and a couple of folding chairs, as well as areas for vehicle inspection and parking. Each of the main buildings is four stories high and all together BRTA employs 40 officers and 150 staff members. The makeshift offices mentioned above deal with serving public needs, such as distributing and collecting forms, e.g. vehicle registration, ownership transfers, and learner permits. In order to facilitate the vehicle-related services, the BRTA needs to verify national identity cards. Customers are expected to handwrite their information on the forms and submit them to the BRTA staff for further processing. Most of these forms require multiple passport size photographs and notary attestations. I frequently observed *dalals* (middle-men) helping customers fill in BRTA forms. On one end of the BRTA, buildings designed for other uses but now repurposed as offices, such as bank booths with tables set up to collect government fees. The premises are patrolled and guarded by members of the Dhaka Metropolitan Police. Beyond the walls of the BRTA, there is a large mosque and a plethora of small businesses, such as photocopy and laminating outlets, makeshift tea stalls and restaurants, shops to notarize documents, and photo studios that serve the needs of BRTA customers. On any working day, the BRTA premises and the surrounding business areas are packed with vehicles and customers.

BRTA is my only field site where every interviewee or respondent requested anonymity. They directly or passively admitted knowing about the "system," which is a term frequently used at BRTA to refer to the practice of offering a bribe to officials in return for efficient service. My respondent Nilufar observed with sheer frustration that "paying bribes is more efficient than waiting in the long queues for basic services." She defined these basic services as paying bank fees, being interviewed for license exams, or getting their vehicles inspected by BRTA officials. As she expressed her helplessness to bypass such corrupt measures, I realized Dhaka's civil society was aware of such issues, but could do nothing to fix it. At that point, I wanted to explore how this system worked at BRTA.

Instead of keeping electronic records on the computers and cameras provided by the World Bank funds, paper records were preferred. Furthermore, whenever possible BRTA officials preferred using pencil rather than pen to write receipts, which meant the document could easily be changed if needed and traces of change were thus minimized.

I also observed Sohel and his colleagues asking for photocopies of various types of documents, such as copies of an identity card or information on the Blue Book (vehicle registration book), instead of verifying these facts on the BRTA database. Since most of the customers did not own photocopy machines or did not carry copies of such documents with them, they were forced to make a trip to the nearby photocopy stalls for such documents. This arrangement between BRTA personnel and the privately-owned photocopy stalls constituted a financial arrangement. According to Mohammad Nobi, an interview subject, when a customer learned he or she needed to submit photocopies of certain documents, which a customer did not have handy, the BRTA personnel directed the customer to "go to Asad Photocopiers across the wall. If they are busy, tell them Shamshu sent you." The BRTA staff person would then receive a commission from the photocopy stall operator.

While explaining how the system worked, Nilufar pointed out that BRTA staff liked to delay submission of customer applications and thus buy more manual processing time to schedule written exams for new motorists or to schedule vehicle inspections. Thus, Nilufar explained, instead of using the electronic scheduling program, BRTA staff preferred to employ manual processing so that customers would be compelled to offer *ghush* (bribes) to expedite their exam or motor inspection dates. A BRTA employee told me that during the few days of annual auditor inspection, the BRTA staff would use the IT programs for these applications as the World Bank intended.

These instances reminded me of Jonathan Parry's (2000, 27) chapter on the "crisis of corruption" in India where he explores the history of the state and of the idea of democracy in post-independent India where the crippling corruption threatened to discredit India's democracy and stability of the state. Similarly, the prevalence of corruption in Bangladesh today, as I witnessed at BRTA, was perhaps more than it was 30 years ago. In others parts of the country, ranging from village tea stalls to fancy restaurants in Dhaka, I observed people nonchalantly discussing paying bribes to conduct government business that includes obtaining utility access in a new apartment, registering land, and avoiding traffic ticket, among other things. Paul and Shah (1997) coined such corrupt measures as 'retail'—"low-level routine corruption of everyday experience" (Parry 2000, 29).

In order to learn more about the 'system'—a form of 'retail' corruption at BRTA, I became a potential BRTA customer and discovered that the system started with the *dalal* (middle-men). Although *dalals* are not officially part of the BRTA administration, they are found everywhere around BRTA, in parking lots, photocopy stands, by banking counters, administrative offices, and tea stalls. There are over 200 *dalal*s in BRTA parking lots during working hours, all men in their 20s–40s with education varying from primary to secondary levels. They are able to complete official forms, written both in Bengali and English, and work for a fee to arrange documents, make copies, pay bank fees, and collect signatures at various counters and offices at BRTA. Each *dalal* carries multiple cell phones and has various office stationeries and supplies, such as paper clips, stapler, or pencils in their handbags. The seasoned *dalal*s, who were in their forties or beyond, functioned as shadow bureaucrats, acting like corporate relationship managers, often seen sipping tea with labour union leaders or higher BRTA officials at various tea stalls.

Every *dalal* had access to any official or bank teller inside BRTA to expedite things for his clients. While sharing tea during non-working hours outside BRTA premises, I interviewed Abul, a *dalal*, and three of his colleagues. Having a common ancestral root in Comilla region of Bangladesh facilitated a functional alliance among us, so Abul answered most of my questions, while his colleagues nodded their agreement. "Our clients are busy people. We maintain good relations with the officials and tellers to better serve our clients. Our clients are busy and we help them. They leave BRTA happy," remarked Abul to explain his work at BRTA. The *dalal*s explained how BRTA clients bargained to negotiate a price with a *dalal* before hiring him. Bargaining is part of Bangladeshi culture and a vendor (or *dalal* in this context) always asked an inflated price before settling on a lower amount negotiated down by the client.

For example, the driving license renewal fee is BDT 1400, but a *dalal* could ask 50 to 100 percent more from a client. "This rate goes much higher in situations when a motorist urgently needs renewed vehicle papers," remarked Nilufar. *Dalal*s can demand as high as 500 to 1000 percent more money for jobs when a client needs a document within a few hours. If a customer is not willing to pay these system fees he or she may need to spend several hours at BRTA merely to determine where to collect forms and signatures, spend the following day submitting the paperwork, and then have to check back in several days about the outcome of the paperwork. Under these constructed circumstances, the system of bribing is efficient and the motorists of Dhaka adapt to the culture of bribery by constructing social relations with *dalal*s based on cash transactions.

The presence of law enforcement personnel at BRTA makes no difference since, as Nilufar pointed out, "they receive commissions [as perquisites of being in a police uniform] from *dalals*, often to overlook the process." As the ineffectiveness of policy is public knowledge, BRTA staff Sohel and *dalal* Abul acknowledged Nilufar's assessment of the police presence at BRTA. Abul added that, "higher ranking officers in the force are making more money than the *dalal*s outside for overlooking bigger matters." Although it was possible to make a written complaint either to the nearby police station or the Office of the BRTA Chairman, a complaint can potentially generate life threatening consequences. For example, as Abul explained, if a *dalal* talked about another *dalal* or a BRTA staff, this would be considered a breach of *bishwas* (loyalty). If a client made complaints about a *dalal* or a BRTA employee to the BRTA hierarchy, the client would be asked to write a complaint letter. However, "no one will read that letter," Abul stated nonchalantly. Perhaps due to a pre-conceived idea about mismanagement and corruption at BRTA, most clients arrive there with an understanding that going through the *dalal* system is the way to conduct business.

I asked Abul and his friends about their monthly earnings. Abul responded on their behalf:

> I make around twenty or so deals a day; do not get to keep more than 300 *taka* (USD 4) in pocket from every deal though. I have to pay everyone to remain as a friend … everyone, starting from the bank teller to the guards, clerks, vehicle inspectors and the higher up officials. The higher the designation, the higher the *di-ner hissa* ['daily tax'] is for the officers.

While a readymade garment worker makes about USD 37 per month, *dalals*, earning over USD 80 per day (or USD 1800 per month) with limited or no formal education, are receiving very good earnings by Bangladeshi standards. Another *dalal* confirmed this approximate monthly income. I also asked Abul how informal money got distributed and split up within BRTA hierarchy. "The officials bribe other big people to get posted here at BRTA. It is a money-making pit," said Abul. When asked for clarity and examples, Abul dropped names, designations, and amounts that came with those posts while he and his friends smiled. "This is public knowledge," he added.

Each *dalal* has an arrangement with a bank teller who collects government fees and several private banks, such as BRAC Bangladesh Bank Limited, worked out partnership agreements with the Ministry. These banks collected government fees on behalf of the Ministry of Communication and charged a small processing fee. According to Abul, "an arrangement with a bank teller consists of paying some money up front to that teller before the start of banking hours every morning. Paying the teller earns me direct access to a specific teller at any given time of a business day to stop in and pay fees for his clients." Abul further elaborated that each bank teller at BRTA maintained arrangements with a number of *dalals* through such advance payment methods. As a result, during working hours most teller windows were randomly interrupted by walk-in *dalals*, while the waiting time for regular customers grew.

Similar arrangements prevailed elsewhere at BRTA counters, such as vehicle inspection or license renewal. "Bank tellers paid a cut to the office clerks, who eventually paid a major cut to the higher ups to turn a blind eye. Everyone is involved. BRTA staff paid large money to their big bosses [senior bureaucrats and politicians] to get posted here," said Abul. I attempted to make an appointment with the person in charge of BRTA. After my fifth phone call in seven days, I was rudely dismissed by the assistant of the person in charge: "Sir is a busy man and is not available for meeting with a PhD student." In a later section in this chapter I discuss the corruption within the BRTA upper hierarchy.

As I learned about the underground economy at BRTA, I became aware of the role of mobile communication that fed into corruption. *Dalals* and BRTA petty officials frequently used cell phones to send and receive text messages. Aid fund contributors, such as tax-payers in the western countries, needed to know that this was how the use of communication technology complemented the underground economy at BRTA.

I asked Nilufar if she and others knew about the World Bank TA that offered IT resources to make processing time more transparent and efficient at BRTA. "No technology can change BRTA's culture" she responded, adding that, "our politicians and the World Bank bureaucrats know about this [BRTA's underground economy]. They benefit from this, too. I learned from Abul that he and his colleagues, who, in fact, boasted that they could prepare any type of document for any type of motor vehicle from a "duplicate license" (fake license) to a forged engine number for an automobile. When asked what type of customers he serviced, Abul remarked that, "the young men that come to Dhaka for the first time and intend to work as drivers for private cars, are my main clients… [and] university students". I enquired what would happen if the authorities attempted to validate these numbers "That will never happen," Abdul replied, laughing at my naïve question, "many lives depend on this [BRTA's underground economy], no one can change this," he said confidently.

When asked what could be done to improve functions at BRTA, Nilufar remarked, "I will be happy to pay additional service fee to the government if they can offer electronic services efficiently. Because the longer I wait here, the more working hours are lost. The Government loses out on revenue earning due to these leaks in the system." She paused and said in a frustrated tone of voice: "But I do not know if anyone with power in the higher up has the intention to change anything here." Her statements supported a similar conclusion made earlier by Abul when I asked him to explain the conduct of the people who made the most decisions at BRTA:

> [There are] a few political leaders, patron labor union leaders, and local *mastans* ['gang members'] who keep BRTA as it is [a concert of organized corruption], while the external auditors come and go. We also want BRTA to stay as it is because our families back in the village depend on us [for remittances] ... You mentioned about aid and budget. We don't know what that is and how that works.

Unable to make an appointment to interview the head of BRTA, I made unsuccessful attempts to speak to other BRTA executives. Despite submitting written letters explaining the purpose of my request, none of the officers agreed to speak to me. With assistance from Sohel, I tracked down the specific floor and building where most of the senior BRTA personnel worked. I managed to enter that floor while catching an open entrance door before it could close. Walking along the floor unescorted I saw, through an open office door, one senior executive speaking on the phone. Given the close proximity and the executive's loud voice, I could hear him making an overseas call, speaking perhaps to a son or daughter, who I assumed was attending a university overseas. The conversation indicated the other person lived somewhere in North America. I heard the senior executive state: "I will send your tuition money before the start of the semester." Given it was early August, college tuition was due at the beginning of the academic calendar in September. If that was the case, considering it takes approximately USD 20,000 per academic year to study at a college in Canada or the United States, I wondered how a BRTA official, who made only USD 150 a month, could afford to send his son or daughter to a university in the west. My curiosity led to a follow-up conversation with Sohel, who informed me that, "most of their children", indicating the children of the BRTA officers, "study abroad or at local private universities."

I contacted Moinul to discuss my findings at BRTA. "These are common public knowledge," he said instantly. He further commented that the international donor agencies were usually aware of the crippling local corruption but addressing that corruption was not necessarily within their specific project mandate. As a result, they did not interfere; thus, they could not actually support the process of reform that was intended by the aid program. This lack of oversight suggests international donors can become complacent when particular aid commodities are transferred in the aid recipient country. At the same time, such complacency, in conjunction with political patronage inside the aid recipient country, can transform 'retail' corruption into a "crisis of corruption" (Parry 2000, 27), as illustrated through various examples drawn from BRTA. Citing historian Morris-Jones (1964, 62–3), Parry adds,

> The impersonal norms of the modern bureaucratic state apparatus are continually subverted by the particularistic obligations of traditional kinship [client-patron relation]. Or alternatively, the civil servant has not yet quite committed himself to the first, but has opted out of the second, with the result that he feels free to concentrate on the lining of this own pocket. (Parry 2000, 52)

While these instances—crisis of corruption—suggests the weakness of the state, they also provide advantageous to certain social groups that helps to solidify the dual hegemonic alliance.

In this section I focused on a specific example from Bangladesh's public sector, the Bangladesh Road Transport Authority (BRTA), which received the financial support of the World Bank. My findings showed that a lack of oversight sustains an underground economy at BRTA. In the following section, I explore how higher education in Bangladesh has adapted to privatization, by following the prescriptions given by a leading international development agency, the World Bank.

As a low-middle-income country with a large and young population base, Bangladesh holds immense potential for market development and growth (The World Bank 2015). In 1992, considering higher education as the medium for development and progress, with facilitation from the World Bank, the Bangladesh government gave permission to open the country's first private university. As of 2017, the official number of private universities in Bangladesh has increased to 140, with more than half of them in the capital city Dhaka (Nurunnabi 2018, 435; Islam 2017). However, the establishment and function of many of these private universities remains a topic of serious concern.

I argue that there exists a disjuncture between moral philosophy and the blind application of right-wing economic prescriptions in Bangladesh's higher education sector. For example, here is an acute absence of basic student services on campuses, such as classrooms equipped with no technology, no standard libraries, no research facilities, and no placement opportunities. Many of the faculty are part-time employees referred to locally as "rickshaw faculty" because they ride rickshaws from one university to the next to teach, leaving no time for them to interact with students or to monitor disciplinary misconduct, such as plagiarism (Husain and Osswald 2016, 1020). My findings that indicate private university owners run their institutions with the goal of incurring profit.

Between 1971 and 1985, there were only four regular and two specialized public universities in Bangladesh (University Grants Commission 2015). After the collapse of the Soviet Union in the late 1980s, and resulting in the formation of the European Union, policymakers in developing countries, inspired by a free-market system, started to modify higher education practices in their respective countries. Since the early 1990s these visions started to be applied in Bangladesh. Market development strategists construed the large, young Bangladesh population as a pivotal revenue generating opportunity. Such economic motivations resulted in a dramatic shift in the country's post-secondary education landscape (Kabir 2010, 619). These reforms also transformed several established public universities into private institutions; the same reforms led to the establishment of an increasing number of private universities in Bangladesh. In most cases, these reforms were implemented with an aim to increase institutional revenue and profit for the capitalist owners of these universities (Quddus and Rashid 2000).

4.3 Neoliberal Directives in Post-Secondary Education

Since the late 1980s and early 1990s, Bangladesh has applied the World Bank directives in various sectors of the economy, including the agricultural, banking, industrial, and higher education sectors (Nuruzzaman 2004). Building upon that, in 2005, the World Bank identified seven major 'crises' in the Bangladeshi education sector and allocated USD 100 million for the reformation of higher education (The World Bank 2005, 122; Kabir 2010, 622), provided that Bangladesh implement key recommendations offered by the World Bank. One proviso suggested government allocation to the higher education sector be reduced and tuition and other fees be increased. This recommendation was made despite the fact Bangladesh already made a very low investment in higher education. For example, Bangladesh's budget allocation for higher education in 2018–2019 was 11.4 percent, which was 2.09 percent of the country's GDP, while other developing countries in Asia, such as India and Malaysia during 2018–2019 fiscal year respectively spent 3.87 percent and 5.74 percent of their GDP on their education sectors (The World Bank 2019).

Center for Policy Dialogue (CPD), a think tank based in Bangladesh that aims to promote inclusive policymaking in the country, argues that Bangladesh's government increasingly allocates a lower percentage of the national budget to the country's higher education sector. For example, during 2015–2016, the government's plan was to spend 14.3 percent on education sector, but it lowered the education budget in 2017–2018 to 12.6 percent, and further lowered it in 2018–2019 to 11.4 percent (CPD 2019). Although overall spending on Bangladesh's education sector has been increasing, but as a percentage of GDP it has been decreasing, for example, 2.18 percent of GDP in 2015–2016 to 2.09 percent in 2018–2019 (CPD 2019). At the same time, in comparison with other south Asian neighbours, Bangladesh spends only 2 percent of its GDP on education, while Bhutan, Maldives, and Nepal spend on average approximately 5 percent of their GDP on their education sectors (CPD 2019).

Jahan (2018) highlights that the Bangladesh Government keeps lowering allocation for education despite making a signed commitment in the Dakar declaration in 2000 to spend at least 20 percent of the national budget or 6 percent of the country's GDP on education. She further shares that most of the government's budgetary allocation on education is spent on paying salaries for teachers and administrators instead of complementing the much needed allocations for research and investments to improve infrastructures.

I argue that such increments in lowering the country's public education sector facilitates the establishment of privately-owned higher education institutes, while the World Bank requires the Bangladesh Government to increase university tuition fees, student loans, and various cost-recovery measures as well as income-generating measures for the public universities. Critics of neoliberalism in higher education (Kabir 2010, 622), argue the World Bank suggestions further accelerated the privatization of higher education institutions in Bangladesh. Kabir indicates that these recommendations were made around the same time as some European countries, e.g. Germany, made public university tuition free.

Nurunnabi (2018, 437) reports that in developed countries, such as Portugal and Spain, despite the increased number of private universities in the last two decades, these univeristies did not emerge as a result of a new market, nor did they create a new market for more private institutions; primarily because the governments in Spain and Portugal, while supporting privatization, held a firm grip on enacting regulations of the private universities (Amaral and Teixeira 2000, 245; Ubillos 2005, 131). However, these scholars also highlight that many developing countries face similar historical, cultural, and political situations to Bangladesh, as well as the World Bank loan conditions and prescription on privatizing higher education.

Banya (2001, 161) argues that the public higher education institutes in sub-Saharan African countries, as a result of reducing budget in public universities and increasing the number of private higher education institutions, face quality issues, and rising graduate unemployment. He adds the governments in these counties have no control over these private universities over tuition fees and regulations. Collins and Rhoads (2008, 215) interpret findings from Uganda and Thailand and observe that the World Bank's one-size-fits-all solution to privatizing higher education does not work. Similar observations were made about privatized higher education systems in Brazil, Mongolia, Oman, the Netherlands, and Ukraine (Al'Abr 2011, 491; Holzhacker et al. 2009).

Returning to Bangladesh, most of my respondents commented that most Bangladeshi private universities are owned and managed by local elites and former senior bureaucrats who have strong ties to the two main political parties that have governed Bangladesh over the last twenty-five years. I elaborate on the short-term outputs and relevant social constructs of applying neoliberal reforms in the Bangladeshi higher education sector in the following paragraphs.

4.4 Free Market Induced Short Term Outcomes in Bangladeshi Higher Education

The public higher education system in Bangladesh has not only suffered from budget cuts, but also went through political troubles, which translated into longer periods for graduation for the students (Islam 2017). All these factors encourage the students from upper and middle-class families in contemporary Bangladesh to attend private universities instead of public ones. Islam (2017):

> Other than a few specializing in engineering or medicine, all the rest of the 100 or so private universities [out of 140] teach "business" to the larger majority of the students. The business majors in these private universities often exceed 80% of the total enrolled students. Let alone the arts, even the basic sciences are not taught in any of these private universities because they are not revenue earning subjects. Most of these private universities have some "general education" courses to cover the sciences and language or literature but students just need to pass a few courses in these. They are not required to attain any *knowledge* of these subjects, because they will all be seeking jobs in business organizations like the banks, where they, supposedly, do not require the knowledge of the arts and the sciences! Contrast this with the study of business subject in the past, up to the 1970s, when only a few less meritorious students, who could not qualify for the science group or the arts group, would be asked to read these subjects. University of Dhaka would admit only about 30 students a year to the Department of Commerce! (Islam 2017, 12)

However, as shared in the previous section, since early 1990s, the free market-induced development agenda transformed the Bangladeshi higher education sector in various ways. Offering additional courses with the primary intention of generating additional funds for the university was one method thorugh which a neoliberal agenda fundamentally altered higher education in Bangladesh. In 2005, for example, Jagannath University, one of Bangladesh's oldest and most prestigious public universities dating from 1858, became a private institution (Kabir 2010, 626). With an aim to generate additional revenues, the public universities started to offer evening courses. For example, The Institute of Information Technology, Department of Development Studies, and Institute of Statistical Research and Training at Dhaka University began offering short training modules for researchers, practitioners, and professionals (Kabir 2010, 626–627).

Also, given Bangladesh's large and young population base, as outlined in chapter one, the local capitalists foresaw investing in the country's privatized higher education sector as an easy and straightforward way to accumulate further wealth. Unlike in North America, in Bangladesh, private univeristies are owned either by politicians, or politically affiliated business people, or senior bureaucrats—the rich Bangladeshi capitalists. These private university owners had successfully managed to restrict moves towards reform so that owners can retain their authority in operating the business model of the private university.

Nurunnabi (2018, 455) cites one report made by Transparency International, Bangladesh (TIB) to highlight the nature of hegemonic corruption behind the country's higher education industry:

> 29.6% of private universities are run by businessmen with strong political connections with the government. ...during 2012–2013, most of the approved new universities' owners were democratic government (AL) officials, such as relatives of the Prime Minister, the State Minister's wife, the Whip of the Parliament, three AL leaders, a relative of an adviser to the Prime Minister, the Home Affairs Minister, the former Awami Students' (*Chattra*) League President, an Awami League Advisory Council Member, an Awami League lawmaker, and the Minister and Chairman of the Parliamentary Standing Committee on Education.

These examples highlight the influences of hegemony, nepotism, and rich capitalist class in Bangladesh's private education sector.

All these factors contributed, since the late 1990s, to the mushrooming of private universities in Bangladesh. Although specific conditions are required to open a private univeristy and to gain some kind of accreditation, such as developing a permanent infrastructure on at least five acres of land, as of 2010, over 90 percent of private universities in Bangladesh did not have their own campuses (Kabir 2010, 626–628). As of 2017, only twelve of the fifty-one private universities that sprouted up in Dhaka had permanent campuses (The Independent 2017). A World Bank report states, "Most of the private universities have failed to meet the minimum requirements of physical infrastructures, full-time qualified faculty, libraries, teaching aids, and other facilities to provide proper education" (2014, 1). In analysing this report, Nurunnabi (2018, 436) finds, for example, twenty-three out of seventy-nine private universities operate without a vice chancellor. The trustees of these universities have access to excessive powers and they remain indifferent towards forming and following guidelines.

From 1992 to 2008, the licenses of five universities were cancelled due to violation of various basic infrastructural conditions. However, two of these cancelled institutions continued to conduct academic activities with permission of the High Court (University Grants Commission 2009). As shared in chapter six, the licenses for opening up private banks in Bangladesh have purely been political decisions made either by AL or BNP government. Similarly, either Al or BNP gave provisional approvals or licenses to the rich capitalist Bangladeshis to open up new private universities for a five year term. Although in 2009, the licenses of forty-three out of fifty-one of such private universities were expired, they continued to operate. Another five universities, whose provisional approvals expired ten years earlier, in early 2000, also continued to operate. None of these expired universities had the authority to run their academic activities or issue degrees (Kabir 2010, 627). However, "all these universities still managed to enroll students in academic programs," remarked the focus group participants that had requested anonymity. Also, many private universities did not address the concerns raised over inadequate classroom sizes, non-existent research resources, and a lack of qualified and permanent faculty members (The Daily Star 2010).

The private universities that did manage to secure land from the government to build their own campuses are believed, according to three of my interviewees, Arjun Bose, Momena Hossain, and Shafiullah Quader, to have leveraged their close ties to key personnel within the government in order to get that. Although it is difficult to prove, it is likely that the influence of caste and class facilitated privatization in Bangladesh, since in most cases, senior bureaucrats and retired senior officers from the armed forces, with close ties to the owners of the universities, are hired to run respective administrations.

4.5 Euphemisms and Marketing Globalization

During my fieldwork in Dhaka, I frequently came across brochures and newspaper advertisements that highlighted privatized higher education. The following types of advertisements for bank loans appear frequently in Bangladeshi newspapers, on the websites of private banks, and on urban billboards in the streets of Dhaka:

> Better Education is a dream; is the priority of time! Our Education Loan enables parents/guardians/students for those who want to fulfill their dreams. You can avail the loan with competitive rates, convenient features and simple procedures. (Prime Bank 2014: online)

These ads for bank loans to cover tuition and other relevant expenses to earn a bachelor degree from a private university offer to fulfill the hopes and dreams of modernity. The banks highlight the value of receiving a bachelor degree, especially in business subjects, while hiding the interest rate costs for such loan products.

I conducted six focus group discussions with students at six different private universities in urban Dhaka. My respondents talked about the interest rates offered by the banks on their education loan products that ranged between 36 and 40 percent. I could not find any supporting data from local private banks or a private university on the percentage of students enrolled in a private university who obtained loans from private banks to pursue their higher education. I also reached out to the university registrars' office in six such private universities but was informed they did not collect such information on the students.

My main respondents on higher education including, Fahmid, Bose, and Nargis, explained that the owners of private universities and private banks often came from the same families. Such practices of nepotism and mismanagement can create socio-economic inequality (Mosse 2010; Sen 1982). However, despite the threats of debt and inequality, there remains considerable demand from Bangladesh's urban youth to enroll in a private institution over a public one. The main reason is that, despite the criticism, administrators at the private universities offer and finish courses on time, while the quality of teaching and management staff at the public universities has deteriorated over the years. My respondents critiqued the mushrooming of private universities following public university deterioration, remarking that, "the professors hired by the public universities take leaves of absence and then take full time jobs at the private universities."

When I asked students during my 2014 focus group discussions about their interest in the private universities, their responses made it clear that, in urban Dhaka, middle-class youth between eighteen and twenty-eight years of age, view private university education as a symbol of prestige. "It's cool, most of my friends are here," offered a young man in his early twenties. The focus group participants agreed that attending private universities meant being modern but they often felt pressure to fit in by taking loans from relatives or banks so they could enroll at a private university. A young woman participant in the focus group, also in her twenties, stated, "The teachers are better at my private university. The classes start on time and I get my papers back on time. That was not the case at Dhaka's best public university, where I studied in my first year of the university life."

4.6 Rickshaw Faculty

Based on my focus group discussions and observations in these six private universities in urban Dhaka, out of 150 to 200 faculty members, less than 20 percent had tenure or full-time jobs. Of those who were full time, approximately 50 percent were on leave from a public university. As Fahmid pointed out, these instructors take leave from the public universities in order to take advantage of the attractive salaries and quick promotions offered by the private universities. As a result, it was the sessional professors who carried the bulk of the teaching load at the six private universities where I collected data. I also observed that a lack of research facilities, poor remuneration packages, and limited career prospects created a high faculty turnover rate.

I interviewed four part-time faculty members, all men, in their late twenties, at a well-known private university in Bangladesh. They all requested anonymity. They had been teaching at the university between two and four years each but as a collective, they had taught at fifteen to twenty private universities. "I needed the money," remarked one of the men. Another complained about the lack of research facilities as the main reason for planning to leave his teaching job in six months or so. None of these instructors considered that they had enough interaction with students, even to get to know some of their students' names. "I used to take a rickshaw to go to the next university right after I completed my lecture at the previous one. Every day I lectured in at least three or four universities," remarked another. They humorously informed me that it was easy to catch sight of an adjunct faculty on a rickshaw at any time of day in Banani area, new Dhaka's university hub. I later learned that approximately fifteen private universities were located in Banani, which used to be an upper class residential area in the 1970s and 1980s. However, since the mid-1990s, Banani slowly turned into a commercial district. My respondents pointed out to me that many so-called private universities in Banani rented residential houses and multiple floors of a commercial building to function as university facilities. Islam (2017, 12) adds that in Banani there is, "more than one university in one building or more than half a dozen on one street." As of January 2017, only twelve private universities have their own campus and, as I later discovered, the owners of these twelve universities belong to Bangladesh's political elite circles. As I noted above, as well as in chapter six, a few such private universities are owned by former cabinet ministers and political leaders from both AL and BNP, such as Dr. Mohiuddin Khan Alamgir. Also, one such university is owned by a former president of Bangladesh. While nurturing political connections is a necessity to receive permission to operate as a private university in Dhaka, such alliances also provide these universities with immunity from any tangible or perceived inadequacy. Perhaps that is why, despite being a chronic issue within the Bangladeshi private university system, the exploitation of the adjunct faculty members is perpetuated.

Four faculty members is a small sample size and thus inadequate to form authoritative generalizations, however, the issues they faced on a daily basis highlight the commercialization of higher education though privatization and deregulation. Essentially, the massive pools of exploited and under-employed contingent or adjunct private university faculty in urban Dhaka eke out a living by teaching too many courses in too many different universities. They do not have time for students because they have hundreds of them, and are perpetually exhausted. They also emphasize the precarious and dehumanizing experience of belonging to a workforce characterized by low wages (Harvey 2005).

4.7 "McDonaldization" of Culture

Mannerisms, physical gestures, and level of confidence expressed by private university students during focus group communication were different from those of students who attended public universities. Students from private universities perceived themselves as more modern or "western," as reflected in their subtle claims of superiority and higher social prestige. One public university student remarked: "I expect a student from a private university to dress trendy and communicate in English." Indeed, most students who attended private universities opted for western attire, especially jeans, and they liked to eat out, especially western food.

Moreover, for most students, private universities are bastions and producers of privilege, and the various shops that surrounded campuses usually reflected that. Since private university students could easily transfer to a mid-level western university, many such students acted and behaved like they were already in the west. They preferred to have a sandwich and cola for lunch, rather than *bhat-sabji* (rice and vegetables), and checked for Facebook updates on their expensive mobile phones. These private university students who drink cola and eat sandwiches are participating in Western practices because that serves to mark their elite and privileged status. Such behaviors served to differentiate these student groups from those around them.

This Americanization of private university surroundings (and the behavior of students) in urban Dhaka can also be compared to the "McDonaldization" of culture, which George Ritzer (1998, 2, 5–6) defines as "the process by which the principles of the fast food industry are coming to dominate more and more sectors of the world." Ritzer argues that, although McDonaldization has four main dimensions—production efficiency, calculability, predictability, and control—these dimensions also create two undesirable outcomes. First, they create a replaceable work force with minimum abilities for completing simple, focused tasks. Second, McDonaldization creates consumer workers who perform tasks traditionally completed by the company. For example, fast food restaurants encourage customers to carry their trash to friendly receptacles marked "thank you" (Ritzer 1998, 31–34).

I observed the students being well mannered customers at the burger places surrounding private university campuses. The students did not mind taking their trash to the receptacles because doing so gave them a sense of independence and efficiency. I asked some students if they cleaned their dishes or washed their clothes at home. "We have domestics for that," shot back a respondent. I also observed that the McDonaldization process facilitated opening up more burger shops that offered free Wi-Fi in the vicinity of university more than did the book shops, magazine outlets, libraries and photocopy stands combined.

Nargis remarked to me that Bangladeshi private universities instilled a McDonaldization ethos in their students by:

> Creating dependency but not capacity. I have seen many MBA graduates from such universities who can't make a good PowerPoint presentation … From such graduates we will have more consumers and clerks, but

> not anything big ... creating the process of dependency does not lead to progress; it leads to neo-colonization.

Other cultural shifts besides Americanization are present in the private universities. For exmple, Nargis also pointed out that in her recent trips to various private university classrooms she observed the increasing presence of female students in *hijabs*. "I am used to seeing these *hijabis* taking group selfies. I did not know what to make of it because, if you are a *hijabi*, why would you be holding your boyfriend's hand and taking pictures in public place? These are disco *hijabis*. Their veils are for show only." Another respondent, Shahriar Kabir, noted that he grew up in Dhaka in a conservative Muslim family during the late 1950s and early 1960s, a time when few women used *hijabs* and *niqabs*. "But they [women in *hijab* and/or *niqab*] are in abundance in Dhaka at present." Although Nargis and Kabir highlight Islamization in Bangladesh, they interpreted this in most cases to be urban Bangladeshi females, using the *hijab* or *niqab* coverings as a trendy, cultural fashion, rather than as a symbol of their obedience to Islam.

Many urban youths in Dhaka viewed attending private universities for a year or two as an investment and gateway to a university in the west, especially in Australia, Britain, the UK, or the USA. Rich families, or even upper-middle-class families, that could afford to pay foreign tuition would send their children to foreign universities. In fact, splitting time between a local private university and later transferring to a foreign university functioned as a win–win situation for these families and their children.

Sending children to the local private universities for the first two years of a degree and then transferring to a tier-two or tier-three university in the west saved the local families tuition money. Although local private universities in Bangladesh are more expensive than local public universities, the tuition fee in the country's private universities is cheaper than the tuition fees in a foreign university. By using the transfer credit option, the transferring students and their families saved tuition expenses. Second, these students consequently received a foreign diploma, which was prestigious at home in Bangladesh. "When I say I am an Arkansan graduate, that sounds better than saying I graduated from East West University [a private university in Dhaka]," remarked a student focus group participant. In each of the six universities where I held our focus group meetings, students reported that each year approximately 40 percent of students transferred to universities abroad when they reached third year.[1]

4.8 Zombie Graduates

Critics of neoliberalism argue that application of its directives affect the academy paradoxically by creating feelings of compliance and passivity, which included an inability to critical thinking (Beck 2000; Wilken and McCrea 2013). Wilken and McCrea (2013, 29) argue the increasing emphasis on creating a labor force is matched by a decreasing encouragement for independent thought that can be defined as a kind of zombie concept, that is, a living/dead idea that is no longer representative of reality, but can still haunt peoples' minds. This outcome can change the relationship of the student to the university from one of learner to one of consumer, whereby the product they consume is their own educational transformation (Appadurai 1990; Evans 2004, 96; Naidoo and Jaieson 2005). Such transformations tend to negatively impact the students' ability of think and their individual ability to process information and articulate a clear point of view on a given topic.

According to Percy (2011), the concept of zombie graduates ultimately positions students as products of the educational machine complemented by the McDonaldization process, who thus emerge as skilled and qualified bodies that can be put to work in the global knowledge economy as zombie labourers—predictable, replaceable, and subordinate to the corporate establishment (Percy 2011, 29–31). The zombie graduates of such academic processes are likely to suffer from philosophical poverty, that is, someone who is unable to function as a critical reader, writer, or thinker (Husain and Osswald 2016, 1020). Respondents Bose and Shafiullah pointed out, when in the 1970s they graduated from Bangladesh's one of the main public institutions—Dhaka University—not many Bangladeshis could attend university. These respondents believe university education and a diploma had value back then. Presently, despite the abundance of private universities, according to these informants, education and diplomas have lost their value. A free trade and globalization-induced and privatization of higher education in Bangladesh led

[1] I wanted to verify these numbers, as provided by students' personal and anecdotal data, with the office of the registrar in the respective universities. However, each of the registrar offices replied in negative citing privacy.

to the outcomes that subtly displace an individual from agency, cultural roots, and values, to place him or her in a globalized culture filled with corporate commodities (Deleuze and Guatarri 1991). Thus, the production of zombie graduates is a direct outcome of such globally networked process (Friedman 2007; Harvey 2005).

4.9 Betrayal by the Neo-Elites and Intellectuals

In Bangladesh, the bourgeois class owns the means of production and the modes of post-secondary education. The views of my key respondents suggest the Bangladeshi bourgeoisie and the universities owned by them can also create dependency and neo-colonialism in post-independent Bangladesh. My main respondents felt that the alliance between the policy makers and the local bourgeoisie remains the main impediment to sustainable development and growth in Bangladesh. These civil society members remarked that eventually the students in post-secondary institutions need to combine their thoughts and skills with local industry and global market demands. They also expressed their reservations that, "the path to achieve desired results is not a linear one," referring to the importance of multiple perspectives and lack of it in the country's higher education can lead to generating a civil society that is anything but active and vigilant. Particularly, Bose points a finger at the country's intellectuals, such as Dr. Mohiuddin Khan Alamgir ('Chicago Boy') and business leaders for turning into rich capitalists.

In this section, I discussed the privatization of Bangladesh's higher education sector and the deregulation of the public universities in the country in respect to institutional practices, knowledge production and social relations. My findings reemphasize the argument, as illustrated in the previous chapters about how the elites, in alliance with the development industry, control resources in a way that benefits them while disadvantaging the majority of Bangladeshi citizens. Overall, the observations and analysis shared in the chapter lead to the conclusion that development opportunities, despite creating better standards of living for some in the short-run, deepen import dependency and promote economic and social inequality in the long run.

In the next chapter, I weave the connection between neoliberalism and Islam in Bangladesh and reveals specific findings that assist to understand Islam-neoliberal realm vis-à-vis: (a) how Islam in Bangladesh has aligned with neoliberal development, and (b) why then Islamic forces attack foreigners, and "others" in the nation.

References

Al'Abr, Khalaf. 2011, December. "The Impact of Globalization on Education Policy of Developing Countries: Oman as an Example." *Literacy Information and Computer Education Journal* 2(4):491–502. https://doi.org/10.20533/licej.2040.2589.2011.0068.

Amaral, Alberto, and Pedro Teixeira. 2000. "The Rise and Fall of the Private Sector in Portuguese Higher Education." *High Education Policy* 13:245–266. https://doi.org/10.1016/S0952-8733(00)00011-8.

Appadurai, Arjun. 1990. "Disjuncture and Difference in the Global Cultural Economy." *Theory, Culture, and Society* 7(2):295–310.

Bangladesh Road Transport Authority (BRTA). 2014. Last modified 19 March 2014. Accessed 11 September 2014. http://www.brta.gov.bd/index.php/activities.

Banya, Kingsley. 2001. "Are Private Universities the Solution to the Higher Education Crisis in Sub-Saharan Africa?" *Higher Education Policy* 14(2):161–174. https://doi.org/10.1016/S0952-8733(01)00007-1.

Beck, Ulrich. 2000. "The Cosmopolitan Perspectives: Sociology of the Second Age of Modernity." *British Journal of Sociology* 51(1):79–105.

Centre for Policy Dialogue (CPD). 2019. "Education Budget in Bangladesh: An Analysis of Trends, Gaps and Priorities." Accessed 18 March 2019. https://cpd.org.bd/category/policy-briefs/.

Deleuze, Gilles, and Félix Guattari. 1991. *What Is Philosophy?* Columbia University Press.

Evans, Mary. 2004. *Killing Thinking: The Death of the Universities*. London: Continuum.

Friedman, Jonathan. 2007. "Global Systems, Globalization, and Anthropological Theory." In I. Rossi (ed.), *Frontiers of Globalization Research*. Boston, MA: Springer.

Harvey, David. 2005. *A Brief History of Neo-Liberalism*. Oxford: Oxford University Press.

Holzhacker, Denilde, Olena Chornoivan, Demet Yazilitas, and Khishigbuyan Dayan-Ochir. 2009. *Privatization in Higher Education: Cross-Country Analysis of Trends, Policies, Problems, and Solutions*. Issue brief. Institute for Higher Education Policy. https://files.eric.ed.gov/fulltext/ED508091.pdf.

Husain, Matt. 2017. "Aid-Effectiveness: On the Radar and Off the Radar." *Development Policy Review* 35(3):337–348.

Islam, Nazrul. 2017. "Middle-Class in Bangladesh." *Bangladesh e-Journal of Sociology* 14(1) January:4–15. Accessed 27 August 2018. http://www.bangladeshsociology.org/BEJS14.1.pdf.

Jahan, Afrose Chaity. 2018. "Budget Allocations for Health, Education Continue to Shrink." *Dhaka Tribune*. Accessed 18 March 2019. https://www.dhakatribune.com/bangladesh/2018/06/29/budget-allocations-for-health-education-continue-to-shrink.

Kabir, Ariful Haq. 2010. "Neo-Liberal Policy in the Higher Education Sector in Bangladesh: Autonomy of Public Universities and the Role of the State." *Policy Futures in Education* 8(6):619–630.

Katz, Cindi. 2001. "Vagabond Capitalism and the Necessity of Social Reproduction." *Antipode* 33(4):709–728.

Morris-Jones, W. H. 1964. *The Government and Politics of India*. London: Hutchinson University Library.

Mosse, David. 2005. *Cultivating Development: An Ethnography of Aid Policy and Practice*. London: Pluto Press.

Naidoo, Rajani, and Ian Jamieson. 2005. "Empowering Participants or Corroding Learning? Towards a Research Agenda on the Impact of Student Consumerism in Higher Education." *Journal of Education Policy* 20 (3):267–281.

Nurunnabi, Mohammad. 2018. "Accounting for Accountability: A Critical Reflection on the Private Higher Education in Bangladesh." *Administration and Society* 50(3):429–470.

Nuruzzaman, Mohammed. 2004. "Neo-Liberal Economic Reforms, the Rich and the Poor in Bangladesh." *Journal of Contemporary Asia* 34(1):33–54.

Parry, Jonathan P. 2000. "'The Crisis of Corruption' and the 'The Idea of India': A Worm's Eye View." In I. Pardo (ed.), *The Morals of Legitimacy*, pp. 27–55. New York and Oxford: Berghahn Books.

Paul, S., and Shah, M. 1997. "Corruption in Public Service Delivery." In S. Guhan and S. Paul (eds.), *Corruption in India: Agenda for Action*, pp. 144–163. New Delhi: Vision Books.

Percy, Alisa. 2011. "A New Age in Higher Education or Just a Little Bit of History Repeating?: Linking the Past, Present and Future of All in Australia." *Journal of Academic Language and Learning* 5(2):131–144.

Prime Bank. 2014. "Education Loan." Modified 30 May 2011. Accessed 7 May 2014. https://www.primebank.com.bd/index.php/home/education_loan.

Quddus, Munir, and Salim Rashid. 2000. "The Worldwide Movement in Private Universities: Revolutionary Growth in Post-Secondary Higher Education." *American Journal of Economics and Sociology* 59(3):487–516.

Ritzer, George. 1998. *The McDonaldization Thesis*. London: Sage.

Sen, Amartya. 1982. *Poverty and Famines*. New York: Norton.

The Daily Star. 2010. "Amended Law on Private Universities Okayed." Accessed 4 January 2015. http://www.thedailystar.net/newDesign/news-details.php?nid=123568.

The Independent. 2017. "Private Universities—Only 12 Out of 51 Move to Permanent Campuses." Published 19 January. Accessed 9 August 2017. http://www.theindependentbd.com/arcprint/details/77136/2017-01-19.

The World Bank. 2003. "Social Accountability: Stocktaking Exercise for South and East Asia – Website on Infrastructure Projects in Bangladesh." Modified

2003. Accessed 23 September 2014. http://www.worldbank.org/socialaccountability_sourcebook/Regional%20database/Case%20studies%20on%20social%20accountability.pdf.

———. 2005. "Education Sector Strategy Update: Achieving Education for All, Broadening Our Perspective, Maximizing our Effectiveness." http://siteresources.worldbank.org/EDUCATION/Resources/ESSU/Education_Sector_Strategy_Update.pdf.

———. 2015. "Bangladesh Projects & Programs." Accessed 9 January 2015. http://www.worldbank.org/en/country/bangladesh/projects.

———. 2019. "Government Expenditure on Education, Total (% of GDP)." United Nations Educational, Scientific, and Cultural Organization (UNESCO) Institute for Statistics. Accessed 18 March 2019. https://data.worldbank.org/indicator/SE.XPD.TOTL.GD.ZS?end=2018&start=2012.

Ubillos, Javier Bilbao. 2005. "Changing Objectives and Formulas in Privatization Policies: The Case of Spain." *Administration & Society* 37(2):131–167. https://doi.org/10.1177/0095399704273210.

University Grants Commission (UGC). 2009. *Strategic Plan for Higher Education in Bangladesh: 2006–2026*. Dhaka: UGC. Internal document.

University Grants Commission of Bangladesh. 2015. "List of Private Universities." Accessed 9 August 2015. http://www.ugc.gov.bd/university/?action=private.

Wilken, Rowan, and Christian McCrea. 2013. "The Living Dead and the Dead Living: Contagion and Complicity in Contemporary Universities." In *Zombies in The Academy: Living Death in Higher Education*. Chicago: University of Chicago Press.

CHAPTER 5

Neoliberalism, Islam and Intolerance

This chapter traces the emergence and workings of the co-articulation of neoliberalism and Islamism in the domain of state governance in Bangladesh. It aims to explore how the interlinked rise of neoliberalism and religion/Islam produces the conditions for particular outcomes such as "othering" as well as violence against local secular writers and bloggers, intellectuals and critics of "fundamentalism", gay rights activists, as well as members of ethno-religious minorities such as Hindus, Buddhists, and Christians. Considering the lack of scholarly literature on this topic in contemporary Bangladesh, the chapter offers analysis on the relationship between the rising neoliberal state in the 1980s, and with it, the advent of a specific strand of Islamic religiosity that prevails in contemporary Bangladesh. The role of globalization in bringing this about, as well as the exclusionary practices that it creates with respect to other communities, is laid out in this article, which coins the term "the great transformation of Bangladesh" to understand this change, using a lens provided by Polanyi, among others.

Since the beginning of the 1990s, Bangladesh started implementing policies of privatization and deregulation resulting in the broadening of credit and the precarization of domestic labor. Incentives included tax cuts for businesses, some of which were Indian corporations operating in Bangladesh, e.g., Airtel BD, as well as domestic family owned corporate entities, such as *Beximco, Bashundhara*, or *Pran*. An addition to this

M. M. Husain, *Development, Neoliberalism, and Islamism in South Asia*,
https://doi.org/10.1007/978-3-031-03113-7_5

category is the former chief of the army's family venture, *IFAD Group* that, since 2009, has rapidly expanded its presence across business sectors (IFAD Group 2021). In most cases, these neoliberal[1] policies presumed efficiency of the market and went ahead with reducing state interventions in the economy that favored the more subordinate classes (Saad-Filho 2003). Interpreting these developments through a lens that is critical of neoliberalism, the chapter seeks to examine the relationship between these policies and the resurgence of a certain kind of Islamic religiosity that engender inequitable growth, and in which some communities are treated as "others" in the socio-economic system and narrative.

Until two decades ago, it was believed that religion was on the decline and held insignificant space in global politics (Kissinger 1994). However, the influence of religion has risen to play a significant part in today's global world, and is at the pinnacle of international political agendas. Building upon this idea through a critical engagement with interdisciplinary, scholarly literature and fieldwork observations on Bangladesh's social and economic dimensions, this chapter braids Islam and neoliberalism to open up ways of seeing differently. In particular, it examines how global politico-economic structural factors and processes are in conversation with state governments and how that can lead to disparities, fuel differences, and stimulate certain forms of extremism that dangerously reinforce a belief of "clashing" religious and secular worldviews.

The pursuit of the chapter inclines towards studying other largely Muslim countries, such as Turkey, Egypt, and Indonesia. The findings spearhead the exploration of specific discoveries in Bangladesh, namely, how Islam in the country has aligned with neoliberal development, and why Islamic forces appear to attack foreigners, and non-Muslims in the nation. The chapter seeks answers by drawing theoretical influence from-Casanova's (1994) view that market based economic systems de-privatises religion. Gauthier (2019) argues that presently we are in a neoliberal situation in which otherwise inassimilable economics and religion collectively construct emerging phenomena. In addition, Polanyi's (2008 [1944]) ideas of embeddedness and double movement between society, in which religion is a vital component, is used to illustrate the contested strand between Islam and Bengali[2] (Bangladeshi) cultures. I theorize that social relations and production appear to become embedded in Islam instead of Islam being embedded in Bengali cultures (Polanyi 2008 [1944]). I refer to this phenomenon as the "great" transformation of contemporary Bangladesh.

The first section of the chapter lays out the conceptual framework for understanding neoliberalism's symbiotic coupling with Islamism in Bangladesh. The second section offers a comparative narrative on outcomes in regards to the roll out of Islam-neoliberalism in contemporary Turkey, Egypt, and Indonesia. The last section weaves the connection between neoliberalism and Islam in Bangladesh and offers critical analysis.

5.1 Theoretical Influence

The unique, under-theorized topic of Islam-neoliberalism demand to have a specific theory section to unpack the outcome of neoliberalism in Muslim Bangladesh. In his basic critique of neoliberalism, Barber (1996) argues that neoliberal economic theory is the force behind globalization. The author's argument, consequently substantiated by Chang (2003) and Reinert (2007), is that globalization demands, if not rushes, economic and ecological forces to integrate; this can mesmerize developing countries because they are not necessarily equipped with market, resource, information technology, and ecological imperatives to exchange and trade as efficiently as the developed countries. These scholars point out that globalization imposes a culture of its own on a population, thus making local cultures in developing countries feel vulnerable, threatened, and reactive. In particular, Barber (1996) adds that the crises that arise from these are more than economic, and the confrontations often take on a sacred quality for locals. Barber's critique is significant because his concerns are premised upon a logic that reveals that a failure of proper integration of the imperatives can create unregulated market forces that consequently give rise to growing parochial forces in the form of religion, ethnicity, and region, among others. So, it is no surprise that in his conclusion he claims that Islam resists neoliberalism.

Interestingly, scholars including Brown (2006), Dikecx (2006), Connolly (2005), and Gopalakrishnan (2009) explain that it is not only Islam, but other political rationalities, such as republicanism, neo-conservatism and evangelical Christianity in the western world or Hindutva in India, that can also be found in combination with neoliberalism as a "market-political rationality". Karaman (2013) shared a significant body of literature that build upon the conjoining of Islamic values and modalities of neoliberal development in places such as Cairo (Atia 2012) and Beirut (Harb and Deeb 2011). In a parallel vein, this chapter seeks to explain how Islamism and neoliberalism as two distinct political rationalities came to resonate together in the organizational body of the state in Bangladesh.

Casanova (1994) in his explanation of the function of the two distinct political rationalities points out that market based economic systems de-privatize religion. As he puts it: "de-privatisation [...] is the process whereby religion abandons its assigned place in the private sphere and enters the undifferentiated public sphere of civil society to take part in the ongoing process of contestation, disruptive legitimisation, and redrawing of the boundaries" (Casanova 1994, 65–66). Building upon these arguments, Turner (2011) and Gauthier (2019) interpret changes in religious interpretations and perspectives in relation to the outcomes of an economics-led globalization. Turner (2011, 278) explains that such remodeling of religion is deepened by consumerism because it converts religion into lifestyles and voluntary union, rather than belief and belonging-oriented methods. In a similar tone, Gauthier (2019) explains that neoliberalism affects religion through the political and societal stages, such as institutional and organizational levels. However, consumerism affects religion via material conditions, at the level of ethos and cultural ideologies and practices. Alternatively, neoliberalism "impacts and shapes religion from above", while the consumerism acts from "below" (Gauthier 2019, 202). In his words,

> Global-Market regime de-nationalises, transnationalises, de-territorialises, marketises, sometimes re-ethnicises religion within a cultural environment framed by consumerism and market ideologies. The marketisation of religion signifies its transformation along (or against) the structures and dynamics of consumer and financial capitalism, in which the expression of choice is constitutive of subjectivities, identities, agencies, communities, and so forth. ... Marketisation transforms religion into lifestyles, practices, and voluntary adhesion rather than belief and belonging-oriented forms. Marketisation also profoundly modifies religious organisations and their rapport to tradition, whose former modes can be dismissed, challenged, and/or renewed. (Gauthier 2019, 201)

Gauthier's critiques highlight that neoliberalism encourages all organizations, big or small, to perceive themselves on an entrepreneurial model, and to perceive their actions as that of actors within market segments, with an obligation to brand and market themselves and their missions in order to "survive" in a competitive environment (Gauthier

2019, 202). He points out that consumerism commodifies in the opposite direction, in which consumer goods offers meanings, authenticities, and identities competing for choice. As he puts it, "consumerism profoundly changes how social actors engage in religion, and how 'religious resources' become mobilized for producing and expressing identities and constructing meaningful lifestyles" (202). Building upon this, Gauthier (2019) contradicts Barber's (1996) views that claimed Islam resists neoliberalism. Gauthier argues that presently we are in a neoliberal situation in which otherwise inassimilable economics and religion, in particular Islam, collectively construct emerging phenomena. Such constructions render a non-commodity as a commodity and part of a lifestyle, such as knowledge, water, or life itself. Finally, Gauthier concludes that neoliberalism and consumerism are theoretically distinct processes but at the same time both are paradigmatically coextensive with complementary sets of processes.

The last pillar of this chapter's theoretical framework encompasses Polanyi's (2008 [1944]) embeddedness and double movement between society and market that helps to explain how Islam is used as a vehicle for economic development in Bangladesh. Polanyi (2008 [1944]) argues that the entire tradition of modern economic thought is based on the concept of the economy as an inter-locking system of markets that automatically adjusts supply and demand through the price mechanism. He points out that before economists invented the free market system, the human economy, since the dawn of time, was always embedded in society. Polanyi argues that the system of self-regulating markets has subordinated society to the "logic" of the market. As a result, the self-defined "developed" [neoliberal] world now runs society "as an adjunct to the market, where instead of the economy being embedded in social relations, social relations are embedded in the economic system" (Polanyi 2008 [1944], 24). This concept will help to ask if the system of self-regulating markets has subordinated Bangladeshi society to the "logic" of the market, in which identity formation and social relations are represented through consumerism, lifestyles, and voluntary unions under the overarching symbols of Islam, such as fashionable hijab, stylist beard, and brand apparels (e.g., classic kurta for men and shalwar kameez for females), rather than Islamic philosophy and inclusive-oriented wisdom.

Integrating these three theoretical frameworks: Casanova (1994), Gauthier (2019), and Polanyi (2008 [1944]) in the context of Bangladesh poses significant challenges. First, as briefly mentioned earlier, scholarly literature that connects neoliberalism and consumerism in studying Islam in Bangladesh offers considerable limitations. Second, to explore the intersections of neoliberal-Islam in Bangladesh requires a broader focus because traditionally Bengal as a region is known for its multiple *jati-shotta* or nationalities that existed in the land before the arrival of Islam as well as co-existed and evolved with Islam for the last eight-hundred-years (Roy 2014 [1983]; Eaton 1993). Acknowledging these limitations, my theoretical framework attempts to provide a critical lens to understand two seemingly unrelated contemporary phenomena in Bangladesh: absorption of wealth on the one hand, and an increase of marginalization on the other, which leads to growing socio-economic inequality and finally, drastic outcomes such as attacking the so called "others" in the nation.

5.2 Islam-Neoliberalism in Contemporary Turkey, Egypt, and Indonesia

According to Islamic scholar Tahir Zaman, most cases of Islamic responses to "the challenge of neoliberalism to date has been characterized by simply inserting Islam within a capitalist framework through a selective reading of Islamic jurisprudence" (Zaman 2014, online). He came across examples, in particular, from Turkey, Egypt, and Indonesia where the interests of conservative Islam appear to be married to powerful business interests. The author also shared his observations on the energy-propelled, autocratic Gulf states, where "an increasingly consumer-driven culture casts a pernicious shadow over social relations wherein a hierarchy of humanity fixes migrant labour drawn from populous nations in south and east Asia firmly on the lowest rung" (Zaman 2014, online). The author argues that political articulations of Islam acknowledge the significance of class struggle in the lives of ordinary Muslims. These articulations make us aware of the potential harmful implications of unbridled competition and caution against the impulse of modernity with its unremitting drive towards acquisition and accumulation. However, since the late-nineteenth century, and for the best part of the twentieth century, capitalist forces have tirelessly engaged a proliferation of Muslim intellectuals, political activists, and movements with the burgeoning ideas of "socialism" (Zaman 2014). Consequently, Islam's rather reactionary responses to capitalism largely subsided.

Beginning with Turkey, the section below shares the implantation of neoliberalism in other Muslim countries including Egypt and Indonesia to better understand the relationship between domestic processes of socio-economic change and political conflict in tandem with global institutional structures and processes of capital accumulation. These macro findings are distinctive and significant, but limited with respect to information on the advent of consumerism in these economies.

Gönenç (2019) explains since the neoliberal transition in the 1980s, Islamic symbols and references in Turkey became increasingly articulated in the state's ideology premised upon the fusion of domestic, Western, and Gulf capital interests. Together, they contributed to the rise of the Islamist bourgeoisie in the country (Doğan 2013, 291). "The Islamist bourgeoisie refers to certain fractions of bourgeoisie that use Islam as a system of norms and values to regulate relations between labour and capital, and intra-capital relations" (Gönenç 2019, 5; Hoşgör 2015). Gönenç further explains that both the Islamist and Westernized bourgeoisie, which developed and maintained organic and dependent relations with Western capital and "paid lip service" to Turkey's constitutional principle of secularism (Öztürk 2011, 109), supported the Islamization of state ideology. The product was an uneven spatial reproduction in urban and rural areas, and within the urban sections. In urban areas, workers faced significant and suppressing deindustrialization, reduced real incomes, and curtailment of labor rights, despite some organized resistance against the neoliberal restructuring (Atılgan 2012, 351). In rural areas, while smallholders were turned into agricultural workers in their own lands through contract farming, large masses of peasants lost work as a result of privatization of agricultural state-owned enterprises, removal of agricultural cooperatives, and seizing of lands. The majority of peasants and smallholders were forced to migrate to urban areas and became a precarious labor force, often subcontracted by especially the Islamist bourgeoisie (Gürel 2015, 337).

Such migration further resulted in an increase in unproductive labor in urban areas, which maintained relations with rural areas in the form of seasonal agricultural workers (Boratav 2014, 72). This unproductive and/or underemployed labor was often mobilized with Islamism due to the lack of class-consciousness and organization (White 2002, 233). Gönenç (2019) argues that the neoliberal restructuring of class relations was detrimental to subordinate classes in urban and rural areas, thus requiring the strengthening of political Islam to veil class antagonisms and suppress the subordinate classes. Therefore, the subordinate classes in rural and urban areas remained increasingly vulnerable to the influence of political Islam.

Compared to Bangladesh, Turkey is a unique transcontinental country that is home to a number of different cultures and ethnicities. The former is not composed of mainly one homogenic group either, considering the variety of indigenous languages spoken all over Bangladesh, along with a number of dialects of the Bangla language. One or two specific cultural groups in Bangladesh speak Urdu as well. Many of the findings from Turkey are applicable in the context of Bangladesh, such as neoliberalism giving rise to Islamist bourgeoisie, further deepening the urban–rural disparity, creating more underemployment, and making subordinate classes in rural and urban areas increasingly vulnerable to the influence of political Islam. At the same time, the country's privileged social, political groups, along with the Islamist bourgeoisie, veil class antagonisms while suppressing subordinate classes by overplaying the influence of founding fathers and political Islam.

Findings from Egypt cast a similar picture. Joya (2020) offers a critique of market-oriented economic reform policies in Egypt implemented at the order of the International Monetary Fund (IMF), the World Bank, and a rising faction of neoliberal-oriented capitalists within Egypt's former ruling National Democratic Party (NDP). Although her critiques point out the significant role that international financial institutions (IFIs) and domestic actors played in shaping the conditions that led to the Egyptian popular uprising of 2011 and continue to influence political and social conflicts, Joya argues that Egypt's chronic socioeconomic problems need to be situated in a broader context of the country's transition toward authoritarian modes of neoliberalism in the wake of the foreign exchange debt crises of the late 1980s or early 1990s and the water-shed "structural adjustment" agreement with the IFIs. She discusses the adverse social impacts of neoliberalism, detailing the particular spaces within which citizens have been pushing back against neoliberal transformation. Joya argues that authoritarianism has been part of how neoliberalism unfolded in Egypt, which, with the financial support from international backers, reoriented the state to use its coercive power to appropriate values and public funds by forcing liberalization, privatization, and marketization. The logic driving neoliberal policies has been the premise that the growth generated from the private sector and free market-based development would achieve strong economic growth and sustainable reduction in poverty. Joya's research, however, reveals the opposite, which is a typical impact of trickle-down economics.

For example, as shared, by the end of the 1980s, economic crises forced the state to press forward with far-reaching structural reforms recommended by the IMF and the World Bank. These reforms have primarily supported capital accumulation by the propertied and trading classes at the expense of peasants, workers, and the urban poor, pushing many people into the informal economy. Growing poverty and inequality in Egypt occurred simultaneously with higher economic growth, particularly through the 2000s, which Joya argues is the normal functioning of neoliberal development strategies that result in unequal distribution of wealth. Here Joya utilizes Harvey's (2003) theory of "accumulation by dispossession," which is an extension of Marx's writing on primitive accumulation, to provide insights into how law and policy reforms, as well as changes in land tenure and trade liberalization, produced violent dispossession processes that were "necessary" to establish the conditions for capital accumulation in Egypt (Joya 2020, 68).

Moreover, the author points out that the Muslim Brotherhood attempted to institutionalize an Islamic economy as an alleged third way between Western capitalism and socialism or communism. The idea of an Islamic economy signified an attempt to subordinate capitalism to a traditional body of Islamic ethics (and *shari'a*) including the rejection of the "possessive individualism" that forms the basis of Western capitalism. These include prohibition on the payment or taking of interest on loans and mainstreaming *Zakat*, a voluntary tax to finance private, religiously administered charitable programs in opposition to the welfare state, and Islamic inheritance laws that prevent the concentration of property (Joya 2020). However, El-Sherif (2014) argues that the Brotherhood's inclusion in Egypt's political system did not lead to its democratization. The Brotherhood also failed to either appease or successfully confront institutional power bases and the secular elites that were aligned to typical neoliberal mechanism.

Joya (2020) also examines the evolution of the Egyptian military into a dominant faction of the capitalist class with an autonomous institutional power within the context of Egypt's post-colonial capitalist development. She notes that through active engagement in the economy, the military increased its economic role in exchange for staying out of politics, instead accumulating power and wealth through strong ties to investors and major economic powers such as the United States and Saudi Arabia (Joya 2020, 119). Overall, these examples evoke a broad-based discussion regarding the significant role the Egyptian state and IFIs have played in the process of facilitating capital accumulation by polarizing wealth distribution and access to economic resources. This finding is quite relevant to the discussion of Bangladesh.

Finally, in contemporary Indonesia, the most notable assemblage of Islamic and capitalist ethics is termed a “spiritual economy” (Rudnyckyj 2009, 106). This concept is in contrast to the “occult economies” that treat religious resurgence as a refuge from the disruptions wrought by a global “culture of neoliberalism” (Comaroff and Comaroff 2000). As Indonesia faced a new political economic landscape increasingly characterized by transnational competition, the state employed a top-down approach reasoning that by cultivating the religious virtues of the workforce, it could increase productivity, reduce corruption, gear towards international benchmarks, and in the process train employees for privatization of state-owned enterprises. The training sessions for this “spiritual economy” drew on a stirring and often heavy mix of Qur’anic recitations, business leadership training, Islamic history, and popular psychology. This training program, known as “Emotional and Spiritual Quotient [ESQ] Training,” invokes both Islamic tradition and Euro-American management knowledge in the interest of creating a more disciplined employee work ethic (Rudnyckyj 2009, 104). According to Rudnyckyj (2009), the concept of spiritual economics elucidates how two domains, religion and capitalism, are brought together to create a new ethical orientation toward oneself, one’s work, and one’s collectivity. “Islam is not merely a vehicle in this process, as spiritual reform is taken to both enable Islamic virtue and effect dispositions that enhance corporate productivity and competitiveness in an increasingly global market” (107).

Evidence from literature review and general communication indicates that the government of Bangladesh is yet to employ a top-down “spiritual economy” approach to train its government personnel and national labor pool based on the guidelines of Islamic ethics and western professional accountability. However, a version of the ESQ initiatives used to be practiced by the personnel at the banking, medical, academic, and NGO organizations owned or run by the Islamic bourgeois. However, arguably, the state made a more than moderate attempt to break up the country’s Islamic bourgeois, who was their political opponent, and this may have curtailed the rhythm of the course of ESQ expansion in Bangladesh.

A comparison of the findings from Turkey, Egypt, and Indonesia indicate that in Bangladesh, neoliberal outcomes generated an absorption of wealth on the one hand, and an increase of marginalization on the other, leading to growing socio-economic inequality. The process presumed efficiency of the market and inefficiency of the state and went ahead with outlawing state interventions in the economy in favor of the subordinate classes (Saad-Filho 2003, 7). Interestingly, except for a few unrelated events of terrorism in Indonesia, the other two Muslim countries did not necessarily encounter "othering" of religious minorities as an outcome of the neoliberal process that we observe in Bangladesh. This is where the contextually specific dynamics of Bangladeshi nationalism comes into play and is explained in the following section, which begins with a discussion of the emergent consumerism in the country that was induced by economic globalization.

5.3 Islam in Neoliberal Bangladesh: Analysis and Discussion

Before digging deeper into unweaving the relation between Islam and neoliberalism in Bangladesh, this section highlights few quintessential characteristics of Bengali culture. According to Lewis (2011), the complex blend of religion, culture, and language is the catalyst for the country's unique socio-cultural and political formations. However, since the arrival of wide-spread neoliberalism and the subsequent consumerism in the country, Bengali cultures and Bangla language have been influenced far more rapidly by varieties of external forces than they were earlier, for example, during the "Pakistan period." As a result, social and economic relations have started to rely heavily on religion, particularly Islam, as an attempt to produce a new kind of "authenticity" in the country's cultures and language. Scholarly research on this theme also reveals tensions around Islamophobia triggered by the so called "War on Terror" and other forms of stigmatization of Islam may contribute to the overall trend towards Islamic orthodoxy in Bangladesh (Peek 2005; Schmidt 2004; Siddiqi 2019). A comment from a male informant, government official in this context stands out:

> When I grew up in Dhaka in a conservative Muslim family during late 1950s and early 1960s, hardly any women I knew like my mother, aunts, neighbours and classmates used *Hijabs* and *Niqabs*. But they [women in

> Hijab and/or Niqab] are in abundance in Dhaka. ...Bangladeshis want to be Islamic so that their culture and identity do not disappear. (personal communication, August 11, 2016)

Arguably, this reminds us of Hegel's (1979 [1807]) definition of nationalism, which is premised upon the need for people to feel proud of where they come from, to identify with something beyond merely their own achievements and to anchor their identities beyond the ego. Although group identities in Bengal have long been fluid and influenced by various structural forces—political, religious, and economic, the formation of the Bangladesh nation as an imagined community (Anderson 1991) has been fraught with ideological ambiguities in determining the role of secularism and religion in the democratically elected government. While it would be naïve to think that social divisions did not exist in the past, what is apparent is that communal consciousness in Bengal was heightened by certain "investigative modalities" that became central to political legitimization and governance in colonial South Asia. These modalities include the formalization of an "official" historiography, land surveys, census enumerations, surveillance, and curatorial practices (Cohn 1996). Through these "cultural technologies of rule" (Cohn 1996), communal identities and ethno-religious differences were reified by the imposition of western educated, Macaulay-oriented knowledge production, conjoined with new modes of governmentality. In using the term "communalism," the author refers to a particular form of identity construction in the Indian subcontinent that emerges from a nexus of colonial discourse and state practice that involves the "othering" of religious communities (Rahim 2007). In Rahim's words, "Dividing communities along religious lines not only produces a binary political and social division, but also diffuses intra-community contradictions, creating an aura of homogeneity within the rank and file of the community in question" (556).

Building upon that, initially, as shared, the Awami League (AL) government in 1972, under Sheikh Mujib's leadership, enacted a constitution that recognized equal status to all religions, and launched a moderate socialist program to encourage opportunities for social mobility and development that was not available under the Pakistani regime. In support of the constitutional ban on communalism and religious discrimination, the AL government in 1972 declared Bangladesh a People's Republic, picked a national anthem composed by Tagore, and designed a flag completely devoid of Islamic symbolism (Kabir 2007). Geopolitically, the early 1970s was the waning years of the Cold War and the beginning of Western led neoliberalism.

> The country [Bangladesh] found itself entrapped in Cold War proxy politics. The United States, which in a bid to renew relations with China had actively supported West Pakistan during the 1971 war, initially refused to recognize Bangladesh's sovereignty; it was also profoundly suspicious of what it saw as the nation's overtly socialist bent. (Siddiqi 2018, 244)

Thus, it was not a surprise when Muijb's period of relative optimism in the wake of independence, followed by famine in 1974 caused by various natural and human-made conditions (Sen 1982), led to a series of CIA supported military coups in 1975 (Chossudovsky 2003, 161). Siddiqi (2018, 254) marks that period as one when Bengali cultural majoritarianism started to attain a distinctly "Islamic" bent.

Siddiqi's remarks foreground the military coup that brought General Zia-ur Rahman and his Bangladesh Nationalist Party (BNP) to materialize a twin desire to de-nationalize the economy through private capital incentives and to establish a pro-Islamic government. In 1977, as shared, General Zia amended the national constitution by replacing a commitment to secularism with *Bismillah-ar-Rahman-ar Rahim*—the supreme confidence and faith in almighty Allah as the base of all actions. General Zia also added a new clause to Article 25(2) stating the state shall endeavor to consolidate, preserve, and strengthen fraternal relations among Muslim countries based on Islamic solidarity (Siddiqi 2018). Secondly, within the period of 1977 and 1979, General Zia withdrew the ban on religion-based political parties with several executive orders. This gave Bangladesh Jamaat-e-Islami (BJI) recognition as a political party, and it consequently became the county's biggest religion-based political party (Khan 2019). These constitutional amendments fostered transnational ties with other Islamic countries, especially Saudi Arabia. It was not until the assassination of Mujib and Zia's accession to power that the Royal Saudi government formally recognized the new state of Bangladesh. This change of regime "expedited the flow of aid from the Middle East, with Saudi Arabia as the most important source" (Kabeer 2011, 149).

Following his assassination in 1981, as also shared, Zia was succeeded by General Ershad and his new Jatiya (National) Party, a conservative political party that through the Eighth Amendment in Article 2A declared

Islam the state religion of Bangladesh. Ershad also established a *Zakat* fund under the President and made the call to prayer mandatory before all television broadcasts (Kabeer 2011, 147). Backed by a powerful military, including the dispersion of military representatives in various central and local government positions, Islam was given a central place in state ideology as secular and liberal opposition were marginalized (Sobhan 1984, 202). During Ershad's rule, development policies, as influenced by Western neoliberal prescriptions, drifted further to the private sector and export-oriented growth, and economic dependency on OPEC countries such as Saudi Arabia increased (Chossudovsky 2003, 161).

Building upon these macro-level changes, the implementation of neoliberal policies in Bangladesh initiated a surge of commodification of public or commonly held goods including education, water, and health-care, and ushered in a consumerist individualism (Gauthier 2019; Polanyi 2008 [1944]). For example, various aspects of Bengali cultures, such as *Pohela Boishakh* (Bengali New Year) appear to be celebrated with embellished commodification. In addition, *Eid-ul-Azha* (Qurbani Eid) and regular lifestyle have been affected by this phenomenon. In particular, among the people of urban Dhaka, eating out and outsourcing food related responsibilities to catering services have become a common trend. In the words of a seasoned female informant,

> when I was a child we rarely ate at restaurants, we had our clothes tailored and had houses that were very small in comparison to now and they held few clothes, the changes that happened in the 80s, 90s, etc. altered the quality of life - people went abroad more, donors were widespread, financialization spread, people began to migrate to cities. (personal communication, July 13, 2021)

Moreover, I came across a number of crowded "hijab boutique" stores in Dhaka that sold hijab and related accessories and attire. This was a striking discovery compared to a decade-old Dhaka I knew of. In addition, online outlets for "Islamic clothing" appeared on Bangladesh's social media platforms. At the same time, in Dhaka's social scenes, increasing number of females show up with full-sleeve outfits and headgears. This was also an interesting finding because during my lived experience as a child and teenager in the 1980s and until mid-1990s in Bangladesh, I did not come across such consciousness regarding an Islamic identity in social gatherings. According to a university educated, practicing Muslim female informant, "*ghomta* (hijab) in Bangladesh these days represents more like a fashion or a trend than representing an individual's moralistic views and religious expression". In another social event, I heard an elderly female relative listening to a conversion that included "diamond embedded hijabs." These examples of de-privatized faith remind me of Gauthier's (2019, 201) arguments that neoliberalism facilitates producing and expressing identities and constructing meaningful lifestyles through marketization of religion. It converts religion into lifestyles and voluntary union rather than belief and belonging. These practices can profoundly modify institutions and their rapport with tradition, whose former modes can be dismissed, challenged, and/or renewed.

Gauthier (2019), in his explanation of such emerging phenomena, highlights the interconnection between diaspora communities with the effects of emigration, multiple communication technologies, and the global financial system. He argues that in contemporary times, the diaspora remains strongly tied to their communities and homelands. Moreover, it functions as an influential agent for economic development and "in the on-going religious revival" (210). For example, many members of Bangladeshi diaspora around the world also function as influential agents for "the on-going religious revival" through, for example, mainstreaming halal meat consumption and online Quran classes for children, while making contributions for the economic development of the country (Gauthier 2019; Turner 2011). An informant mentioned the "contribution" of migrant workers to this emerged phenomenon. It is important to acknowledge that remittances earned by Bangladeshi migrant workers contribute significantly to the economic development of the country, and they remain underappreciated and marginalized both at home and abroad. However, the wife and elder daughter of a migrant worker, who was present at the time of my informal chat with his family, mentioned that "*Uni* [the husband] after returning home from *Arob desh* [the Middle East] encouraged me and my daughter to wear *niqab*."

Kibria (2008) explores the identity transformations of Muslim Bangladeshi labor migrants to the Gulf states of the Middle East. She explains that for the Bangladeshis, developments of national consciousness, in particular of a critical nationalism, remain a key feature of the migration episode. The migrants affirm the *ummah*—the idea that the bonds of Muslims, based on their adherence to the core tenets of Islam, are far more important than differences of culture and nationality. In addition, Gardner and Osella (2004) highlight that the intertwining of religious practice and consumption in this process: "as migrants and their families reinvent themselves as high-status members of their community, how they worship and how they spend their earnings – activities which are often closely linked – tend to take centre stage" (xxxiii). Kibria (2008) further elaborates that "in an assertion of modernity, the returned South Asian migrant rejects the local folk Islam of his/her home community in favor of a global and 'pure' Islam" (521).

Whether through diaspora or local consumerism, a certain emerging phenomenon brought in a more conservative strain of Islam that is being enforced at the socio-political and individual level through consumerism in the name of preserving the "authenticity" of Bangladeshi Muslim culture. For example, Griffiths and Hasan (2015) in their study of rural *madrassahs* in Bangladesh found that these institutions frown upon women's empowerment and openly preach men to enforce wearing *hijabs* and *niqabs* on women. During my general communication with farmers, owners of small business, and laborers, I observed that Bangladesh's urban and rural bourgeois establish new mosques and madrassahs in their rural constituencies and encourage others to donate to these establishments. It is argued that this Islamism veils the struggle of unproductive and/or underemployed labor and their lack of class-consciousness and organization (White 2002).

During the trips to rural Shirajganj and Munshiganj districts, as well as during a trip to Cox's Bazar, I came across loud speakers in bus stations, rickshaw stands, and market areas that continuously played *waz mahfil* (Islamic sermons), preaching the benefits of following the five pillars of Islam, and praising Prophet Mohammed for his conduct in educating the masses. In the first two locations, which were purely rural settings, I noticed such sermons often involved giving vulgar, misogynistic speeches regarding females, and derogatory comments about "others," rather than discussing the five pillars of Islam. For example, in Bangladesh's social media, a fraction of speakers in *waz mahfils* events claim self-coined rhetoric, such as "women are born to pleasure males" and "Allah wouldn't punish a Muslim when he seizes the property of a non-Muslim" (*Bangladesh'r Rajniti* 2021, online). Stille (2020), based on fieldwork and interviews, analyzes an archive of several dozens of sermons, and argues how popular preaching shapes roles and rules of what can be said, imagined, and felt. He adds that since the nineteenth century, *waz mahfils* have become so popular that today it is possible to participate in them on a daily basis in many regions of the country. Despite their significance in the rise of popular politics, the sermons are often disregarded as Islamist propaganda, and very little research is dedicated to them.

Although reasonable Bangladeshi Muslims reject any propaganda-filled *waz*, the role of the state in tracking down the ill-educated preachers, who apparently have large number of followers, is unclear. These were surprising discoveries for me because growing up as a male in the late-80s and early-90s, I witnessed *waz mahfils* as indoor events for special Islamic occasions, in particular, before Friday's *Jummah* prayer. However, what I witnessed two decades later suggested Islam had become de-privatized (Casanova 1994). Moreover, the money or "donation" collection aspect of these stalls reminds of Gauthier's (2019, 202) critique that neoliberalism encourages all organizations, big or small, to perceive themselves on an entrepreneurial model, and perceive their actions as that of actors within market segments, with an obligation to brand and market themselves and their missions in order to "survive" in a competitive environment.

Citing these measures as examples of "creeping Islamisation," Schendel (2009, 38) argues that they polarize a Bengali vernacular cultural model (and traditional identity) with more "authentic" Islamic religious conduct, now considered pious by villagers and many in the country's urban sphere. This can be explained as globalization imposing a culture of its own on the Bengali population, and through this, the market dominating the three main cultural elements: language, culture, and religion, in particular Islam (Barber 1996; Casanova 1994). Thus, an emerging phenomenon is constructed, in which otherwise unassimilable economics and religion coexist to complement sets of processes (Gauthier 2019). I argue that in contemporary Bangladesh, the development of a majoritarian, nationalistic discourse of Islam is an outcome of an emerged phenomenon (Gauthier 2019), in which social relations and production have become embedded in Islam instead of Islam being embedded in the larger culture (Polanyi 2008 [1944]). I refer to this phenomenon as the "great" transformation of Bangladesh. Explaining how this has materialized in the span of two decades is a challenging task (Fig. 5.1).

Quadir (2015) provides an alternative that can be contextualized in the de-privatization of Islam in Bangladesh. He explains that politicized and unaccountable state practices have unleashed a wave of privatization [neoliberalism] that suggests that politics has become the main vehicle for accumulating capital in contemporary Bangladesh. For example, close

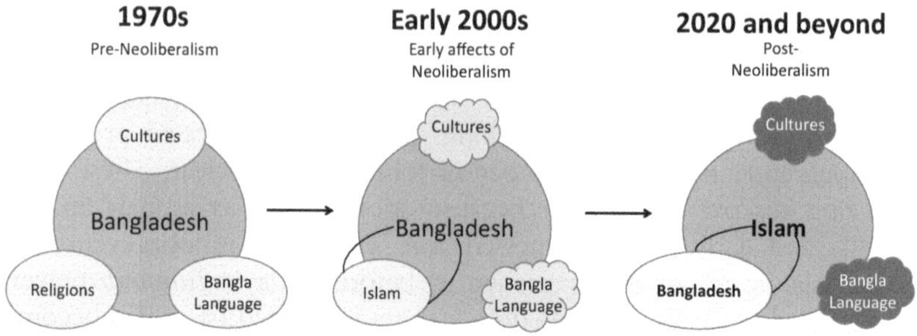

Fig. 5.1 Bangladesh—The "great" transformation (*Source* Author's own formulation)

ties between government bureaucrats and businessmen turned party loyalists has led to a surge in granting operating licenses to start private banks, private television channels, and private universities in the country (Amundsen 2016; Ruud 2011). Political patronage is the most critical component in this context, and has also been known to protect the members of party student wings, trade union groups, and grassroot party volunteers (Lewis 2011; Riaz 2014; Ruud 2011). In this context, Ahmad adds,

> But one of the biggest challenges which we did not understand, confront or defeat was corruption. It did not remain a set of discrete criminal acts; it gradually became a way of life that engulfed us, practiced openly and boldly. (Ahmad 2021, online)

In principle, a version of such reconfigured client-patron relations existed before this new phase of capitalism, but its newly emerged form under neoliberalism fostered conditions for disaffection and desperation, presently leveraged through the provision of free healthcare, education (e.g., Qur'anic schools) by Islamic political parties, such as the *Bangladesh Jamaat-e Islami* (BJI) and others including *Hefazot e Islam* and *Islami Oikya Jot* (Islamic Unity Front) (Riaz 2012, 2014; Tasnim 2012; Mishra 2013). Casanova refers to such instances as a de-privatizing moment for a religion because this is how Islam in Bangladesh abandons "its assigned place in the private sphere and enters the undifferentiated public sphere of civil society to take part in the ongoing process of contestation, disruptive legitimization, and redrawing of the boundaries" (Casanova 1994, 66). In addition, Lewis (2011) critiques such client-patron relations in that they created a space for Islam that was consequently used for political expediency. Lewis's conclusion echoes Riaz's (2004) findings that ascendant conservative Islamization is the outcome of a deliberate act of economic and political partnerships that have been in function in Bangladesh for the last 25 years.

According to Rosenblum (2003), what we come across in Bangladesh has resonance in other multi-religious countries, such as India and Israel, where religious political parties have gained prominence in recent decades through the marketing of specific religion(s) by providing concrete material benefits such as new schools, daycare facilities, and housing projects (Turner 2011; Gauthier 2019; Gopalakrishnan 2009). She argues that through this "associational nexus," religious parties such as *Jamaat-e-Islami* in Bangladesh combine political activities with social development, and treat society as subordinate to the economy. This is what Polanyi highlights as the self-defined "developed" world running society "as an adjunct to the market, where instead of the economy being embedded in social relations, social relations are embedded in the economic system" (Polanyi 2008 [1944], 24). In addition, Riaz (2004) argues that under an overarching political umbrella, this has emboldened student members, trade union leaders, and grassroot party volunteers to employ a "politics of fear" for capital gain. He points to radical branches of these parties that recruit vulnerable, desperate and marginalized young minds, and draw them into the so called "Islamic forces" that consequently attack "others" in the nation. Prominent Bangladeshi filmmaker Tareque Masud (2010), in his award-winning feature film *Runway*, showcased this recruitment aspect of Islamic extremism in Bangladesh.

Unfortunately, the religious demography in Bangladesh has changed considerably in recent decades. The most salient demographic trend is the declining number of Hindus in the country. At the time of Bangladesh's independence in 1971, the Hindu population amounted to approximately 23 per cent of the country's entire population. Current estimates put that figure at around nine per cent (Sunandapriya 2013). There are a number of factors and motivations contributing to this migrant outflow. Two critical dimensions noted by the UN special report were the role of contested property relations between Hindu and Muslims, and the experience of harassment, and at times, physical violence towards religious minorities (UN 2015, 6–7). In the words of a male, aged mid-40s, informant:

> Bangla language, Bangladesh is my ancestral right and land but as a Hindu minority, frankly speaking, I do not always feel safe. Most Bangladeshi Muslims are kind and warm but I have come across a few odd, Islami radicals like RSS or BJP-esque. When you have small children at home, you need to feel assured. So, I, like many other Hindu families in Bangladesh, managed *Aadhaar*[3] cards for my family as a backup in case we ever need to move to India to save our lives. (personal communication, August 24, 2016)

In addition, in the Chittagong Hill Tracts region, where the religious landscape has distinctively differed from the rest of Bangladesh, demographic changes have been even more pronounced, not least as a result of government-induced population resettlement, particularly since the late 1970s (UN 2015). Unlike a few decades ago, when the indigenous peoples living in that region—mostly following Buddhism and Christianity—constituted the vast majority, the proportions of indigenous and Bengali populations have by now become more or less even. As a result of those changes, Islam has become quite visible in the shape of many newly erected mosques and *madrasas*, similar to the rest of Bangladesh. Findings from field observations indicate remittances from the Middle East and the influence of global Islam have significantly contributed to this spatial transformation (Kibria 2008). In addition, the northwest of Bangladesh, where many Hindu and indigenous groups have been living for generations, has started to experience religious violence, in particular Islamic extremism (World Watch Monitor 2015; European Country of Origin Information Network 2018). This has resulted in the migration of many Hindu families to the Chittagong Hill Tracts region, where they feel safer than in other parts of Bangladesh (UN 2015). It should be noted that, in this region, ethnic and religious minorities, although largely overlapping, are not identical. For instance, some of the Buddhists or Christians living in the region have a Bengali background, while the majority of the followers of those two religions are indigenous from the Chakma, Marma, Tanchangya, and Khyang tribal groups. Despite these common cultural histories and ties, religious minorities in Bangladesh have faced threats of displacement, harassment, and violence. Siddiqi (2019) adds, "For the hypernationalist and authoritarian state, I contend, queer and politically dissident bodies are equally disposable" (2).

Unfortunately, certain patterns that emerge from the above case of the Hill Tracts indicate that religious minorities suffer from displacement, forceful out-migration, and continue to feel insecure and vulnerable in Bangladesh. Feldman (2016, 2) maps how intertwined processes—"a set of ongoing and contradictory policy reforms and practises that reproduces both difference and majoritarian rule"—made Hindus as national "others" and dispossessed them of their land in contemporary Bangladesh (Qutb 2006 [1964]; Rahim 2007). Informal conversations with Bangladeshi academics, human rights activists and retired high ranking military personnel show that they acknowledged the correlation between the political agenda and violence induced displacement of religious minorities in Bangladesh that is often driven by economic motives and has accompanied the broader shift towards unregulated markets and increased privatization. Essentially, this confirms Harvey's (2003) theory of "accumulation by dispossession" in the case of Bangladesh, a version of which Elyachar (2005) and Joya (2020) cited as a neoliberal outcome in contemporary Egypt.

These examples suggest a peculiar, uncalled for outcome of forceful materialism under a neoliberal umbrella that appears to be legitimized by employing Islam. However, if we interpret the two key concepts, *Rabbaniyat* and *Khalifat*, as explained by Hashim (1965, 33) and Huq (2013, 56), to know and live Islam means is to sustain one's own self and other creatures around him or her faithfully. These scholars further explain that a Quranic exegesis mutes the question of religious culpability of non-Muslims and highlights one to focus back to the self, whereby any human being, through uncontrolled material desires and an ill-directed use of power, can deny god. Therefore, what we can presently observe in Bangladesh in the name of Islam, can be explained as an emerging phenomenon induced by neoliberalism and consumerism (Gauthier 2019).

Although ethno-religious minorities have borne the brunt of this Islamization within the changing landscapes of Bangladesh, they are not the only ones feeling marginalized and dislocated. Other ethnic minorities, local secular writers and bloggers, intellectuals and critics of Islamic fundamentalism, and gay rights activists—that challenged the rise of extremism and fundamentalism—have also faced discrimination in recent decades. This has been, in particular, apparent among the country's growing youth population. These examples reemphasize that neoliberalism and consumerism are two different, but complementary, sets of processes. In addition, the examples affirm that modernity includes land as a commodity, and neoliberalism deepens that trend. Overall, they indicate a marketization of Islam that in the last few decades triumphed at the cost of fueling ethno-religious conflict and communal tensions in Bangladesh.

This chapter attempted to weave the connection between neoliberalism and Islam in Bangladesh by illustrating how an overarching theme of neoliberal development brought in a commodity culture through privatization and an increased consumerism and carved room for Islamic symbols to form identity for the locals. The chapter also provides arguments in favor of the existence of a certain kind of patron-client setup that employs "Islamic forces" to attack "others" for capital gain and terrorizes foreigners.

I anticipate readers will confer that Bangladesh is at a crossroads after its 50 years and in the twenty first century. Despite tremendous potential for economic growth, it has done little to protect, let alone strengthen, the legal rights and freedoms of religious minorities that was part of the bedrock of its constitution. This is not unique to Bangladesh. It is well known that the state's involvement in religious life under a neoliberal umbrella remains a contentious one in Bangladesh, elsewhere in South Asia, and around the world. Arguments and evidences presented in this chapter do not indicate that the Islamization of Bangladesh foreclose the possibility of a just and moral society, nor do they intend to reinforce the common trope that Muslims are somehow resistant to secular ideas. Rather, the explanations indicate, as Max-Neef (2012) puts it, "neoliberal economics which has conquered the entire world backed by most politicians and corporate people is killing more people than the armies put together" (online). Finally, when ascendant forms of religious nationalism emerge alongside economic policies that foster conditions of socioeconomic inequality and marginalization, they create conditions where violence and extremism thrive. The question moving forward is not that religion should be taken off the agenda in political and public life in Bangladesh, but rather what are the best practices for thinking about civil society where there can be positive cooperation between religious views and the state (Calhoun et al. 2011).

Notes

1. A new phase of understanding of the politics of development began in the 1970s when the Bretton Woods financial institutions imposed structural changes in the modern era that ultimately changed the meaning of development, especially for those countries trapped by these new arrangements. For example, these international financial donor institutions removed the control of the state on capital that consequently weakened the capacity of a state to promote national economic growth. At the same time, the dominant economic players encouraged increased cross border capital flows. These changing policies are frequently defined as neoliberalism. See Harvey (2005), Chang (2003), Husain (2019), Reinert (2007), and Venugopal (2015) for details.
2. Bengali culture is based on the material conditions—agriculture, food, weather, and climate, among others, for the ethnic *Bangla* (Bengali) speaking peoples living in the Ganges Delta region of the Indian subcontinent. Rivers, boats, monsoon, agriculture, and folk music, among others, are the backbone of the Bengali culture. Bengali people speak in various dialects of the Bengali language. Traditionally, rivers form as boundaries as to where one dialect will begin and another will end (e.g., people on both sides of the *Padma* River speak in two different dialects of the Bengali language). Various historical and political events and influences divided the Bengali culture into two countries: West Bengal province in India and to the east, Bangladesh. This consequentially led to the construction of two cultural capitals for the Bengali culture: Kolkata (previously, Calcutta) in West Bengal and Dhaka (previously, Dacca) in Bangladesh. In the twenty-first century, Bengali culture has expanded globally to the various corners of the world due to emigration. At the same time, this culture appears to be slowly disappearing vis-à-vis other dominant South Asian cultures based on Hindi and Urdu languages. Moreover, the influence of English language and culture, as a result of colonization, remains strong in the region. Collectively, one can argue that these external cultural influences, as they mix with various external economic and political forces, subtly cause a sense of insecurity among the Bengalis (collected from anonymous interviewees).
3. *Aadhaar* means "foundation" or "base." In the context of India, the term refers to a 12-digit unique identity number for the residents or passport holders in India, based on their biometric and demographic data. Presently, *Aadhaar* is the world's largest biometric ID system. Ref: https://uidai.gov.in/about-uidai.html.

References

Ahmad, Ahrar. 2021. "The Politics of Anti-Politics: Corruption, Democracy and the Universities." *The Daily Star*. 8 July. Accessed 22 July 2021. https://www.thedailystar.net/views/opinion/news/the-politics-anti-politics-corruption-democracy-and-the-universities-2124751.

Amundsen, I. 2016. "Democratic Dynasties? Internal Party Democracy in Bangladesh." *Party Politics* 22(1):49–58.

Anderson, Benedict. 1991. *Imagined Communities: Reflections on the Origin and Spread of Nationalism*. London: Verso.

Atia, M. 2012. "A Way to Paradise: Pious Neoliberalism, Islam, and Faith-Based Development." *Annals of the Association of American Geographers* 102(4), 808–827.

Atılgan, G. 2012. "Türkiye'de Toplumsal Sınıflar: 1923–2010." In Faruk Alpkaya and Bülent Duru (eds.) *Türkiye'de Toplumsal Yapı ve Değişim*, pp. 323–366. Ankara: Phoenix.

Barber, B. R. 1996. *Jihad vs. McWorld: How Globalism and Tribalism Are Reshaping the World*. New York: Ballantine Books.

Boratav, K. 2014. *Türkiye İktisat Tarihi 1908–2009*. Ankara: İmge.

Brown, W. 2006. "American Nightmare: Neoliberalism, Neoconservatism, and De-Democratization." *Political Theory* 34(6): 690–697.

Calhoun, Carig with Mark Juergensmeyer, and Jonathan Van Antwerpen. 2011. *Rethinking Secularism*. London: Oxford University Press.

Casanova, J. 1994. *Public Religions in the Modern World*. Chicago: University of Chicago Press.

Chang, Ha-Joon. 2003. *Kicking Away the Ladder: Development Strategy in Historical Perspective*. London: Anthem Press.

Chossudovsky, Michel. 2003. *The Globalization of Poverty and the New World Order*. Quebec: Global Research.

Cohn, B. S. 1996. *Colonialism and Its Forms of Knowledge: The British in India*. Princeton: Princeton University Press.

Comaroff, J., and J. Comaroff. 2000. "Millennial Capitalism: First Thoughts on a Second Coming." *Public Culture* 12(2):291–343.

Connolly, W. E. 2005. "The Evangelical-Capitalist Resonance Machine." *Political Theory* 33(6), 869–886.

Dikeex, M. 2006. "Two Decades of French Urban Policy: From Social Devel opment of Neighbourhoods to the Republican Penal State." *Antipode* 38(1), 59–81.

Doğan, A. E. 2013. "İslamcı Sermayenin Gelişme Dinamikleri ve 28 Şubat Süreci." In İlhan Uzgel and Bülent Duru (eds.), *AKP Kitabı: Bir Dönüşümün Bilançosu*, pp. 283–306. Ankara: Phoenix.

Eaton, Richard M. 1993. *The Rise of Islam and the Bengal Frontier, 1204–1760*. Berkeley: University of California Press.

El-Sherif, A. 2014. "The Egyptian Muslim Brotherhood's Failures." Published on 1 July 2014. Accessed 6 May 2021. https://carnegieendowment.org/2014/07/01/egyptian-muslim-brotherhood-s-failures-pub-56046.

Elyachar, J. 2005. *Markets of Dispossession: NGOs, Economic Development, and the State in Cairo*. Durham: Duke University Press.

European Country of Origin Information Network. 2018. "Bangladesh: Freedom of Religion or Belief." Published September 2018. Accessed 12 May 2021. https://www.ecoi.net/en/file/local/1447985/3175_1540665654_2018-09-general-briefings-bangladesh.pdf.

Feldman, Shelly. 2016. "The Hindu as Other: State, Law, and Land Relations in Contemporary Bangladesh." *South Asia Multidisciplinary Academic Journal* 13(13). https://journals.openedition.org/samaj/4111.

Gardner, K., and F. Osella. 2004. "Migration, Modernity and Social Transformation in South Asia: An Introduction." In F. Osella and K. Gardner (eds.) *Migration, Modernity and Social Transformation in South Asia*, pp. xi–xlviii. New Delhi and London: Sage.

Gauthier, F. 2019. "The Marketisation of Religion." In *Religion, Modernity, Globalisation*. London: Routledge.

Gönenç, U. 2019. "Charity State: Neoliberalism, Political Islam, and Class Relations in Turkey." *New Proposals: Journal of Marxism and Interdisciplinary Inquiry* 10(1) April:16–28.

Gopalakrishnan, S. 2009. *Neoliberalism and Hindutva: Fascism, Free Markets and the Restructuring of Indian Capitalism*. Delhi: Aakar Books.

Griffiths, Martin, and Mubashar Hasan. 2015. "Playing with Fire: Islamism and Politics in Bangladesh." *Asian Journal of Political Science* 23(2):226–241.

Gürel, B. 2015. "Türkiye'de Kırda Sınıf Mücadelelerinin Tarihsel Gelişimi." In Sungur Savran, Kurtar Tanyılmaz, and E. Ahmet Tonak (eds.), *Marksizm ve Sınıflar*, pp. 303–385. Istanbul: Yordam.

Harb, M., and L. Deeb. 2011. "Culture as History and Landscape: Hizbullah's Efforts to Shape an Islamic Milieu in Lebanon." *Arab Studies Journal* 19(1), 12–45.

Harvey, David. 2005. *A Brief History of Neo-Liberalism*. Oxford: Oxford University Press.

Hashim, A. 1965. *As I See It*. Dacca: Islamic Academy.

Hegel, G. W. F. 1979 [1807]. *Phenomenology of Spirit*. Oxford: Oxford University Press.

Hoşgör, E. 2015. "Islamic Capital." In Neşecan Balkan, Erol Balkan, and Ahmet Öncü (eds.), *The Neoliberal Landscape and the Rise of Islamist Capital in Turkey*, pp. 142–165. New York: Berghahn Books.

Huq, Samia. 2013. "Defining Self and Other: Bangladesh's Secular Aspirations and Its Writing of Islam." *Economic and Political Weekly* 48(50):51–61.

Husain, Matt Mustahid. 2019. "Who Reaps the Benefit?—Dual Hegemony and the Politics of Development in Bangladesh." PhD thesis, University of British Columbia.

IFAD Group. 2021. "Management." Accessed 21 July. http://www.ifadmultiproducts.com/about/.

Joya, A. 2020. *The Roots of Revolt: A Political Economy of Egypt from Nasser to Mubarak*. Cambridge: Cambridge University Press.

Kabeer, Naila. 2011. "The Quest for National Identity: Women, Islam and the State in Bangladesh." In Kamala Visweswaran (ed.), *Perspectives on Modern South Asia: A Reader in Culture, History, and Representation*, pp. 139–153. Malden: Wiley-Blackwell.

Kabir, Shahriar. 2007. *Cultural History of Secular Humanism in Bangladesh*. Dhaka: Dana Printers Limited.

Karaman, O. 2013. "Urban Neoliberalism with Islamic Characteristics." *Urban Studies* (Edinburgh, Scotland) 50(16):3412–3427.

Khan, H. M. 2019. "The Changing Face of Political Islam in Bangladesh: From Compromise to Confrontation? (1991–2016)." *Journal of Bangladesh Studies* 21(2):45–59.

Kibria, Nazli. 2008. "Muslim Encounters in the Global Economy Identity Developments of Labor Migrants from Bangladesh to the Middle East." *Ethnicities* 8(4):518–535; 097077. https://doi.org/10.1177/1468796808097077.

Kissinger, H. 1994. *Diplomacy*. New York: Simon and Schuster.

Lewis, D. 2011. *Bangladesh: Politics, Economy and Civil Society*. Cambridge: Cambridge University Press.

Masud, T. 2010. "Runway." *Bangla Movie*. Accessed 4 September 2015. https://youtu.be/cVHr6tMpU_I.

Max-Neef, M. 2012. "Keynote at Zermatt Summit." Accessed 1 July 2020. https://www.youtube.com/watch?v=5EURJI9x9Qs.

Mishra, Pankaj. 2013. *From the Ruins of Empire: The Revolt Against the West and the Remaking of Asia*. Toronto: Doubleday.

Öztürk, Ö. 2011. "Türkiye Finans Kapitalinin Dışa Açılması." *Devrimci Marksizm* 13–14:106–132.

Peek, L. 2005. "Becoming Muslim: The Development of a Religious Identity." *Sociology of Religion* 66(3):215–242.

Polanyi, Karl. 2008 [1944]. *The Great Transformation: The Political and Economic Origins of Our Time*. Boston: Beacon Press.

Quadir, Fahim. 2015. *Civil Society in Asia: In Search of Democracy and Development in Bangladesh*. Aldershot: Ashgate.

Qutb, S. 2006 [1964]. *Milestones*. The Mother Mosque Foundation. Cedar Rapids, IA.

Rahim, Aminur. 2007. "Communalism and Nationalism in Bangladesh." *Journal of Asian and African Studies* 42(6):551–572.

Reinert, Erik. 2007. *How Rich Countries Got Rich and Why Poor Countries Stay Poor*. London: Constable.

Riaz, Ali. 2004. *God Willing: The Politics of Islamism in Bangladesh*. Oxford: Rawman and Littlefield.

———. 2012. *Inconvenient Truths About Bangladeshi Politics*. Bangladesh: Prothoma Prokashan.

———. 2014. *Culture of Fear: The Political Economy of Terror and Violence in Bangladesh* (in Bangla). Dhaka: Prothoma Prokashan.

Rosenblum, N. 2003. "Religious Parties, Religious Political Identity, and the Cold Shoulder of Liberal Democratic Thought." *Ethical Theory and Moral Practice* 6(1):23–53.

Roy, A. 2014 [1983]. *The Islamic Syncretistic Tradition in Bengal*. Princeton: Princeton University Press.

Rudnyckyj, D. 2009. "Spiritual Economies: Islam and Neoliberalism in Contemporary Indonesia." *Cultural Anthropology* 24(1), February:104–141.

Ruud, A. E. 2011. "Democracy in Bangladesh: A Village View." In S. Toft Madsen, K. B. Nielsen, and U. Skoda (eds.), *Trysts with Democracy: Political Practice in South Asia*. London and New York: Anthem Press.

Saad-Filho, A. 2003. "Introduction." In Alfredo Saad Filho (ed.), *AntiCapitalism: A Marxist Introduction*, pp. 1–26. London: Pluto.

Schendel, Willem van. 2009. *A History of Bangladesh*. Cambridge University Press.

Schmidt, G. 2004. "Islamic Identity Formation Among Young Muslims: The Case of Denmark, Sweden and the US." *Journal of Muslim Minority Affairs* 24(1):31–45.

Sen, Amartya. 1982. *Poverty and Famines*. New York: Norton.

Siddiqi, Dina. 2018. "Secular Quests, National Others: Revisiting Bangladesh's Constituent Assembly Debates." *Asian Affairs* 49:1–21.

______. 2019. "Exceptional Sexuality in a Time of Terror: "Muslim" Subjects and Dissenting/Unmournable Bodies." *South Asia Multidisciplinary Academic Journal* 20(20):online. https://doi.org/10.4000/samaj.5069.

Sobhan, Rehman. 1984. *The Crisis of External Dependence: The Political Economy of Foreign Aid to Bangladesh*. London, UK; Bangladesh: Zed Press University Press.

Stille, M. 2020. *Islamic Sermons and Public Piety in Bangladesh—The Poetics of Popular Preaching*. London: Bloomsbury Publishing.

Sunandapriya, B. V. 2013. *Attacks on Buddhists: Ominous Inaction*. Dhaka: Sougata Prakashan.

Tasnim, Eshita. 2012. "The Minority Protection." *The Daily Star*. 20 October. Accessed 12 August 2016.

Turner, B. S. 2011. *Religion and Modern Society—Citizenship, Secularisation and the State*. Cambridge: Cambridge University Press.

United Nations (UN). 2015. "Report of the Special Rapporteur on Freedom of Religion or Belief on His Visit to Bangladesh." 9 September 2015. Accessed 5 August 2016. http://www.ohchr.org/Documents/Issues/Religion/A-HRC-31-18-Add2.pdf.

Venugopal, Rajesh. 2015. "Neoliberalism as Concept." *Economy and Society* 44(2):165–187.

White, J. 2002. *Islamist Mobilization in Turkey: A Study in Vernacular Politics*. Seattle: University of Washington Press.

World Watch Monitor. 2015. *Attack on Nuns Said to Be First Ever in Bangladesh*. Published 12 August. Accessed 12 May 2021. https://www.worldwatchmonitor.org/2014/08/attack-on-nuns-said-to-be-first-ever-in-bangladesh/.

Zaman, Tahir. 2014. "Political Islam in Neoliberal Times." *OpenDemocracy*. 17 November 2014. Accessed 5 May 2021. https://www.opendemocracy.net/en/north-africa-west-asia/political-islam-in-neoliberal-times/.

CHAPTER 6

Neoliberalism and the Political Economy of Bangladesh Military

This chapter aims at understanding the entrepreneurial engagements and ventures undertaken by Bangladesh Armed Forces through its welfare wings: *Sena Kalyan Shongstha* (SKS 2022) and Army Welfare Trust (AWT). The objective of the chapter is to produce a self-evident empirical exercise that establishes the link between military resources and its contributions in Bangladesh by focusing on the military's resource accumulation through commercial activities, such as development and state-building. To have an idea of how deep Bangladesh's military resource network is, the chapters looks at three distinct levels: (a) small and medium enterprises run independently by units and divisions. These businesses range from gas stations to more intensive ventures; (b) public sector large enterprises—this refers to organizations like the *Sena Kalyan Shangstha* that is run under a formal public sector set-up; and (c) large-scale private sector ventures (university, five-star-hotel, etc.) where some or all of the resources have been drawn from the public sector. Usually these activities are undertaken by the civilian private sector.

Given the restrictive nature of data source, I acknowledge at the outset that the findings for this chapter are limited, preliminary and do not portray a generalized narrative. In addition, given the complex post-independence history of Bangladesh, as briefly shared in Chapter 3, the country's socio-political system has evolved to allow the ruling elite to cohabit with the military, which has also evolved into an independent class.

M. M. Husain, *Development, Neoliberalism, and Islamism in South Asia*, https://doi.org/10.1007/978-3-031-03113-7_6

Arguably, Bangladesh presently has a one-party, 'democratically' elected government, which cannot exist without military support. The country's political and business elites apparently built an informal partnership with the military, and this chapter explores whether the military's involvement in commercial activities benefit a select few, and results in cost for the public sector that are usually not included in the defense estimates. The answers to these queries are important because there are other countries with extensive military engagement with private sector enterprises, such as Pakistan, Turkey, and Indonesia. However, in terms of Bangladesh, the issue is that there is a lack of understanding of how the entanglement of (senior) officers with links to the state may seek to alter the operation of the state because of their private sector interests.

According to Siddiqa (2011), from the perspective of a transitional democracy, Bangladesh can seemingly boast of a good track record of pushing the military out of politics. Despite its chaotic politics, the armed forces are firmly under the control of the civilian government. However, the apparent strengthening of democracy in the country also indicates a fundamental shift in civil–military relations. The military seems to have conceded civilian supremacy in exchange for the political governments ensuring the security of the organization's corporate interests. Building upon Siddiqa's analysis, I interpret this evolving relation resembling a dual-hegemony model (Husain 2019), in which the state is both the military's patron and client at the same time, which results in benefitting both the state and the military. As a result, the military in Bangladesh these days enjoys a well-earned credence and prominence in terms of its share of the economic resources of the state but not necessarily in the country's power politics. The military's status as an equal partner in running specific economic sectors and mega-projects are owed to the particular nature of civil–military relations, which can be explained by looking at the history of the evolution of the Bangladeshi state.

6.1 Theoretical Influence

> Civil–military relations are rather about how military force is relevant to the political goals of the stakeholders than an issue of control. The military is essentially a policy tool, and how it is utilized by the ruling class depends upon the nature of a country's politics. The way in which the military is deployed, in turn, determines the tenor of the relationship between it and the general public. (Siddiqa 2011, 3)

The precursors for the author's arguments are based on Samuel P. Huntington's *Soldier and the State* and its key role in defining the nature of the relations between militaries and civilian leaderships (Huntington 2005). The existing literature on civil–military relations views the military as a professional force and a corporate entity over which civilian authorities exercise control. Unlike praetorian armed forces that control the political and administrative functioning of the state, a professional military is subservient to civilian control. Essentially, Siddiqa (2011) interprets that Huntington identifies the military's subservience to civilian authority as one of the prerequisites for its organizational professionalism. Other authors, such as Amos Perlmutter, further elaborate upon the concept, firmly linking the military's subservience to political masters as a feature of a liberal or democratic political environment (Perlmutter and Bennett 1980). Although subsequent works by Alfred Stepan (1971) and Morris Janowitz (1988) sought to play around with a re-explanation of military professionalism, Huntington's definition, according to Siddiqa (2011) continues to be significant in shaping arguments about civil–military relations.

However, the author further argues that one of the problems with Huntington's definition is that it does not completely capture the relevance of military force for public policy or the organization's relationship with the state and the civil society.

The theory of concordance, as unpacked by Rebecca Schiff (2009) views civil–military relations through the importance of culture that transcends disciplines, vocations, and organizational establishments. The author presents corporate America as one such context in which culture vitally impacts its internal workings. The precursor for the author's arguments is rooted in de Tocqueville's observations made 170 year ago, in which US citizens in particular enjoy giving back to society (1901: 798). The author interprets this enthusiasm escalate into grander schemes of targeted philanthropic efforts by corporations, many of which participate in the high-profit partnership of the military–industrial complex that considers alternative ways of conducting business and how to affect social change beyond weapons production. During the 1960s and 1970s, both realms embraced the concept of social responsibility: civil–military relations by considering or at least being affected by the impact of indigenous culture on foreign militaries (Vietnam) and Corporate America by considering the changing corporate cultures and thus eventually flattening its hierarchy. Currently, Corporate America is taking new strides to adjust to another dominant cultural trend of the time: to fulfill a humanitarian call through philanthropic and social responsibility efforts. If corporate concordance can help companies align their objectives with the unique structure of the company, then corporate concordance might also become a viable tool for militaries and civilian elites (including corporate leaders) to achieve healthier civil–military relations. In essence, corporate concordance has the potential to move outside the walls of corporations and define and achieve goals relevant to the corporate, military, and civilian relationships. Specifically, the role of corporations could transform from solely internal profit-driven motivations to external humanitarian partnerships with the military, governmental elites, and citizens.

Building upon the theory of concordance and critical interpretation of Huntington's definition civil-military relations, the chapter explores and interprets the findings in Bangladesh, where the civil-military relationship is ever evolving under an overarching neoliberal landscape. Regardless of the politics of the state, business interests, in principle, engages various actors and the involves relationships among the stakeholders. Siddiqa (2011) argues that military's corporate interest under civilian state leadership relationship has emerged due to the civilian leadership's recognition of the military's role in the country's society and politics. This embeds an inherent, reasonable understanding that the best way for providing an exit to the military from politics to ensure and sustain an environment, in which the military's corporate interests are guaranteed by civilian governments (Siddiqa 2011, 32). She finds three factors that determine the extent of the influence that a defense establishment eventually exercises. First, the nature of the political system and the relative strength of others involved is a key determinant. In a state where political forces are weak, the militaries claim greater political space. Second, the character of the military has a bearing on its ability to claim greater political space. Third, political and geopolitical objectives determine the degree of influence exercised by a military.

Exploring answers to these critical queries through an evolving neoliberal phenomenon, in which underprepared developing nations engage in privatization, can be challenging, to put things mildly. Other limitations of the study can include the following: (a) social science research has not systematically looked at the military's entrepreneurial ventures under the neoliberal phenomenon in Bangladesh; (b) while there are availability of rich anecdotal information, this information neither allows for statistical analysis nor support theoretical grounding; (c) the deficiency of organized data has not encouraged researchers or scholars to investigate the genre of limitary capital, nor does the existing literature on civil-military relations and democracy analyze the link between military's public sector engagement and military authoritarianism; and (d) except for Bangladesh, a series of case studies are available on a number of countries that describe the military's business operations or the internal economy. However, they fail to present a cogent and systematic theoretical analysis.

6.2 Key Findings

Today's Sena Kalyan Sangstha is a derivative of the welfare foundation inherited from the Pakistan days when the Fauji Foundation had established businesses in the Eastern wing of united Pakistan. In 1972, Sheikh Mujib, Bangladesh's first prime minister, affectionately known as *Bongo Bondhu* (friend of Bengal) formally inaugurated Sena Kalyan Sangstha for the welfare of veterans and family members of servicemen. He also established *Muktijoddha Kalyan Trust* (Freedom Fighter Welfare Trust) for the welfare of non-military Bangladeshi freedom fighters and their families. Siddiqa adds,

> the actual boost to the military's role in the corporate sector came under the regime of General H.M. Ershad, who encouraged the military's profit-making ventures to acquire financial autonomy for the armed forces. Today, the military is not a significant player in the commercial sector, but its presence in business has been gradually increasing and seems to have grown as a result of the flow of revenue made possible by the UN peace-keeping missions. In fact, the UN peacekeeping missions are an essential part of the Bangladeshi military's corporate interests. (Siddiqa 2011, 26)

One may find it ironical that Bangladesh military's business interests have thrived more under civilian rule than under martial law regimes. For example, in 1998 Bangladesh army established AWT, which is owned and operated by Bangladesh Army. Today, AWT and SKS together have successful business divisions, in particular, SKS operates in: (i) electronics, (ii) cement, (iii) trading and textile, (iv) liquefied petroleum gas, (v) food, (vi) edible oil, (vii) service, such as tours and travel, overseas government to government employment, (viii) real estate, and (ix) information and communication technology. While AWT runs five-star hotels, golf clubs, filling stations, shopping complex, sea port, a commercial bank that as 40 branches around the country and, all in its own land and without accumulating any public resources. These institutions employ a few thousand permanent and contractual staff. The uniqueness of these organizations, in particular, for SKS that it is the first in Bangladesh to implement social business. This substantiates the arguments made by theory of concordance. In addition, SKS never made a loss, while according to informants, *Muktijoddha Kalyan Trust* functions on government subsidy. Another uniqueness of SKS is that despite being a government organization, it has its own budget. A number of SKS operations, in particular, overseas employment program, became so efficient and successful. For example, it provided six-month long plumbing training to 292 civilian men and sent them overseas with guaranteed government jobs. SKS charged each candidate only BDT 35 thousand (~USD 400) that private sector agencies in Bangladesh charge usually seven or eight times more. Despite achieving unprecedented success in a sector Bangladesh is known for notoriety, due to unknown (political) reasons, SKS has been refrained from conducting business in the sector. However, due to popular demand, both SKS and AWK intend to start business ventures in new sectors in Bangladesh.

The successful private sector ventures by AWT and SKS are not beyond criticism. According to Ahmed (2010) from the BBC, "a number of retired generals have expressed their unease over the army's extensive exposure in the fields of trade and industry." BBC also cited a senior public official saying, "Law and order forces are meant for defending the country, they are not supposed to run factories or business units." Despite these concerns, it is reasonable to say that unless public intuitions and corporations in Bangladesh develop any positive credibility in the public domain, the military with its existing sincerity, efficiency and professionalism with continue to grow and prosper in Bangladesh's private sector.

The gradually increasing conservatism and radicalization of the Bangladeshi society, which I refer as Bangladesh's "great" transformation, contributes an overall collective frustration towards the state politics. As a way out, many argue that the military, given its strong credibility in management and getting things done, perhaps can be a suitable contender to protect the marginalized in the country. Other factors, such as an increasing dissatisfaction with India, in particular its subtle arm-twisting and often cold predatorial moves in trade prompt mass sentiment to build an expectation from the military to restore public confidence. Quite interestingly, public sentiment in Bangladesh at the same time moved on from comparing Bangladesh military to that of Pakistan, which often can shadow praetorian characteristics: as Shashi Tharoor once humorously coined, 'other countries have military, but in Pakistan, the military has a country.' Rather, in Bangladesh, despite its shifting client-patron based relation with state governance, the military remains as a disciplined institution and keeps recognizing democracy as a superior value. In turn, this makes state and society view the term 'civil–military' as a value-laden partnership for greater good.

In the next chapter, I summarize my results, analysis and subjective experience. I also offer some insights that can contribute to the improvement of development policies around the world.

References

Ahmed, Kamal. 2010. "Bangladesh Army's Advancing Business Interests." Published 15 August 2010. Accessed 21 June 2021. https://www.bbc.com/news/world-south-asia-10801268.

Huntington, Samuel P. 2005. *Soldier and the State: The Theory and Politics of Civil–Military Relations*. Cambridge, MA: Belknap Press.

Husain, Matt Mustahid. 2019. Who reaps the benefit?—Dual Hegemony and the politics of development in Bangladesh. PhD thesis, University of British Columbia.

Janowitz, Morris. 1988. *Military Institutions and Coercion in Developing Nations: The Military in the Political Development of New Nations*. Chicago: University of Chicago Press.

Perlmutter, Amos, and Valerie Plave Bennett (eds.). 1980. *The Political Influence of the Military*. New Haven: Yale University Press.

Schiff, Rebecca. 2009. "Concordance and Culture from the Military–Industrial Complex to Corporate Philanthropy." In *The Military and Domestic Politics: A Concordance Theory of Civil-Military Relations*. London; New York: Routledge.

Sena Kalyan Shongstha (SKS). 2022. https://www.senakalyan.org/corporate-overview.php.

Siddiqa, Ayesha. 2011. "The Evolution of Civil–Military Relations in South Asia." In E. Sridharan (ed.), *International Relations Theory and South Asia: Security, Political Economy, Domestic Politics, Identities, and Images*, vol. 1. Oxford: Oxford University Press. https://doi.org/10.1093/acprof:oso/9780198069652.001.0001.

Stepan, Alfred. 1971. *The Military in Politics Changing Patterns in Brazil*. Princeton, NJ: Princeton University Press.

CHAPTER 7

Conclusion

I began my monograph by asking why, after forty-seven years of development initiatives that include receiving billions of dollars' worth of aid every year, do so many Bangladeshis continue to be victims of poverty—unable to access basic necessities, such as shelter, water, and sanitation, as well as remain forced to seek employment in sweatshop-like working environments in Bangladesh and beyond to make ends meet? My investigation led to the body of evidence presented throughout this monograph, which outlines the ways in which hegemony, poverty, and underdevelopment are constructed and maintained in Bangladesh. My findings conform in important respects to a broader set of findings and analysis that informs debates about global development in the twenty-first century (Escobar 2012; Ferguson 1994; Frank 1967; Mosse 2005). Much of the literature in which these debates occur confirms that the types of 'development' processes described here routinely benefit only a few social groups, while undermining local cultural values and practices and local economies.

In the paragraphs that follow I will first discuss the most important of my findings as they bear on the general question of why development initiatives in Bangladesh have failed in such profound ways over the full time period of their implementation and why they continue to fail. These include: (a) Bangladeshi's divisive and fractured middle-class; (b) the "dual-hegemony" of state and aid agencies operating in the country; (c) Bangladesh's dependency on foreign imports; and (d) the failure of the

M. M. Husain, *Development, Neoliberalism, and Islamism in South Asia*,
https://doi.org/10.1007/978-3-031-03113-7_7

education system to prepare citizens for participation in a truly democratic state. After describing these four key findings I will return to the three more specific research questions that guided my field research, as outlined in chapter three. I will then offer a few policy recommendations and conclude with a discussion of the limitations of my monograph and share tentative future plans for additional research.

7.1 Bangladesh's Divisive and Fractured Middle-Class

Whereas the Muslim, Bengali middle-class led the inspiration for independence during the Pakistani period, the influence of that group consequently diminished in post-independent Bangladesh, particularly in defining the country's political and economic course. Such a fading role of the Bangladeshi middle-class is tied to the power vacuum that emerged at the end of the Pakistani period. This period facilitated the emergence of a new Bangladeshi elite class (e.g. military and business class) that achieved hegemonic status through forming alliances with the Bretton Woods financial development industry. In the meanwhile, most of the educated, middle-class representatives emigrated as skilled professionals to various developed, Western countries such as USA, UK, Australia, and Canada. As result, Bangladesh middle-class characteristics including education-based value system and work-ethic (e.g. punctuality), as well as cultural practices (e.g. reading English classics, listening to Tagore music) appear to be disappearing among the country's existing so called middle-class, civil society population. More alarmingly, politicization of each category of professionals (e.g. academics, lawyers, and physicians) through patron-client relationships forces special professional groups to ally with one elite group, or political party, and at the same time against another political party. Operationalizing such a patron-client relationship transforms civil society members into clients of the ruling party. Moreover, being able to control the country's military as a client, which has a sobering influence on anyone that wishes to protest, supports the achievement of a hegemonic state. Building upon that, mainstreaming patron-client relationships to run bureaucracy (e.g. government agencies), media, and universities significantly influences the Bangladeshi middle-class, intellectuals, and professionals to remain divisive and fragmented.

My research also supports the conclusion that civil society as a whole in Bangladesh is equally divided and fragmented. The other classes in the country, the poor and unemployed and the organizations, protest movements, and NGOs that represent their interests, also remain fragmented and constrained, and thus unable to act effectively. As a result, these social groups fail to stand united, as well as remain unable to influence the course of national economic and political development. The overall enforcement of patron-client relations impedes the emergence of the intellectual individual, which according to Gramsci (2010) is more important in a society than forming an intellectual class through education. Although these leaders often emerge from the middle class, they can emerge from any class and typically work across class relations. Thus the presence of a dual hegemony functions as the main catalyst behind the fragmented status of the Bangladeshi middle-class population and civil society as a whole.

7.2 Dual-Hegemony of State and Aid Agencies Operating in Bangladesh

I defined dual hegemony as an alliance between the new Bangladeshi political and economic elite class and the Western international aid/development industry. Such a type of hegemony requires both actors—the state and aid agency—to be jointly functional at the same time to be effective; the absence of one makes the other inoperable and unproductive. For example, as demonstrated in chapter five, Bangladesh Government accepted USD 3 billion loans from the World Bank right before the country's general election in December 2018. Considering geo-politics, as well as the US State Department's substantial influence on World Bank's development policies and priorities, I question Bangladesh Government's securing that loan amount right before the general election in 2018. Such a transaction suggests a negotiated pact towards earning a silent buy-in from the US government on the upcoming election outcome.

I infer that the Bangladeshi Government would be unable to remain in power for the following five years in case the US State Department raises question about the conduct of the government's neutrality in managing its various agencies during the election process. At the same time, I also conclude that the World Bank is able to operationalize new income revenues as a result of disbursing the USD 3 billion loan, which was the highest amount of foreign loan in Bangladesh's economic history. While the World Bank could not deliver so without working with the

Government of Bangladesh, the loan transaction indicates how the World Bank—an external force—can continue to be in a position to influence national development policies in Bangladesh, which Chilean economist Osvaldo Sunkel (1972), as elaborated in chapter two, criticizes as a way to make a country dependent and vulnerable.

Overall, as illustrated in chapter three, analyzing the increasing amount of development loans from Bretton Woods institutions in Bangladesh since in 1972, as well as analyzing the fall of the military government that opposed to Western development prescriptions in mid-1980s (Chossudovsky 2003), I attribute the development loan transactions between the Bangladesh Government and the World Bank as an example of "dual hegemony." Achieving state power through dual hegemony enables the new Bangladeshi political and economic elite class to retain its hegemonic status. As a result, the country's middle-class and civil society as a whole continue to remain divisive and fragmented as the authoritarian rulers treat the country's intellectuals, professionals, and impoverished as subordinate classes. This system of patron-client relationships operationalizes divisions on the home front and the pattern of dual hegemony on the international front, benefiting the economic-political elite while creating greater inequalities and ever more entrenched patterns of poverty and migration in contemporary Bangladesh leading to underdevelopment (Escobar 2012).

7.3 Bangladesh's Import Dependency

Bangladesh is yet to fully develop its industrial base as it continues to rely on low-skilled workers in the export-oriented industries, such as the readymade garment industry. These industries continue to import raw materials, for example, according to a World Bank (2018) source, as of 2016 Bangladesh imported (21 percent of GDP) more than it exported (17 percent of GDP), creating a negative trade deficit of approximately USD 9 billion (The World Bank 2018). As elaborated in detail in chapter five, the country's trade imbalance has been rapidly increasing with the greater inflow of foreign direct investments in Bangladesh; most of which are used to finance import expenses (Chang 2003; Chossudovsky 2003; Reinert 2007). These examples highlight Bangladesh's present day economic and industrial dependency on other countries, particularly the industrially advanced Western nations. In all, through these transactions more than 90 percent funds for development aid return to the donor countries in the name of commodity, knowledge, and information transfer. While less than 10 percent of aid resources stay in Bangladesh, such funds go to manage overhead expenses of aid agencies working in Bangladesh, as well as to the local elites and do not necessarily trickle down within the local socio-economy.

Improving the industrial base and skill of the general manpower, as achieved my countries including India and China, can be a source of inspiration of Bangladesh to successfully compete in a free-market economy. As illustrated in chapter two, every major economically rich and technically advanced developed countries, including the United States and United Kingdom, practiced economic policies that protected their national companies during the process of industrial development (Chang 2003; Reinert 2007). These authors conclusively proved that once these major economically rich and technically advanced developed countries had reached a level of industrial development to compete in the global market, they adopted free market approaches. In that context, Bangladesh joined the free-market economy before improving its industrial base. Therefore, examples of economic success of India and China, along with effectively partnering with Bretton Woods institutions can be a way for Bangladesh towards overcoming underdevelopment in the country.

However, given the existing course of 'development' in Bangladesh, the country could suffer from similar extreme outcomes as endured by Germany during the decades after the end of WWI. As explained in chapter two through the Treaty of Versailles that enforced reparation payments of Germany by the Western Allies after the end of WWI, Germany became overburdened with debt, which consequently provided a breeding ground for nationalism and militarism in the country (Urmetzer 2003, 81). At the same time, Germany was unable to adequately engage in the international economy. Urmetzer (2003) draws a parallel to what happened in Germany after the WWI to contemporary Third World debt, much of which is enforced by the IMF and World Bank, as well as remarks that this debt "is likely to produce similar outcomes" (Urmetzer 2003, 87). Such an insight is crucial to understanding the role of the World Bank in the so-called economic development (neoliberalism) of contemporary Bangladesh. Therefore, the importance of improving the industrial base and human capital skills is critical for the country, much of which can be achieved through improving the education system. This was the path implemented by India and China, as I explained in chapter two (Chang 2003).

7.4 The Failure of the Education System to Prepare Citizens for Participation in a Truly Democratic State

Operationalizing neoliberalism in Bangladesh since early 1990s, as outlined in chapter nine, the country's higher education sector became transformed in various ways. For example, while the Bangladeshi public higher education institutions suffered from budget cuts, deregulations in the higher education sector led to the creation of privatized education institutions. That transformation encouraged the students from upper and middle-class families in contemporary Bangladesh to attend private universities instead of public ones. These privatized univeristies are owned either by politicians, or politically affiliated business people, or senior bureaucrats—the rich Bangladeshi capitalists. The politically and economically privileged owners of these private universities had successfully managed to restrict moves towards reform so that the owners can retain their authority in operating the business model of their respective private universities. As illustrated in chapter nine, an increasingly privatized education sector in Bangladesh is failing its students by poorly allocating academic resources. The same sector is also failing the country by undermining the ability of university professors to be advocates for fair dealing, human rights and democracy, as well as by weakening the ability of the middle-class to provide leadership.

7.5 Specific Responses to Research Questions

My interdisciplinary research project sought to answer the following three questions: (a) are aid resources actually reaching their intended recipients, or are the elites capturing or diverting them; (b) how much influence do the members of each of these social groups have in the design of development projects in Bangladesh; and, (c) how aware are the members of each of these development social groups of the effects of development projects in general. Below I specifically answer each of these three research questions based on my fieldwork findings and analytical observations.

I observed that in both rural and urban settings, newly emerged economic-political elites consume most of the resources and exercise decision-making authority on behalf of all Bangladeshis, leaving both the urban and rural middle-class, intellectuals, professionals, and impoverished to function as subordinate groups with no voice in the design and deployment of development in the country. As explained earlier, the newly emerged economic-political elites and their sub-streams of political, military and bureaucratic surrogates control the course of development in Bangladesh, as endorsed by the hegemonic Bretton Woods institutions and their partners that form the entire aid industry. The Bangladeshi local elites also maintain hegemonic status through sustaining its alliance with the Bretton Woods development industry partners. That pattern of dual hegemony in turn creates greater inequalities and ever more entrenched patterns of poverty and migration in contemporary Bangladesh.

In regards to carrying influence in the design of Bretton Woods development projects in Bangladesh, as shared earlier, the impoverished have no voice either in the design or deployment in the country. Although it is difficult to quantify, available evidence indicates that in almost ninety percent of cases most of the development aid resources return to donor countries in the name of technology, commodity, and knowledge transfer. The local elites and their business enterprises benefit from the residual funds through forming patron-client relationships by subjugating the country's other socials groups including middle-class, intellectuals, professionals, and impoverished, among others.

For example, as identified through the case of BRTA, as illustrated in chapter eight, I observed that political leaders, mainly business owners, tend to recruit people from their political constituencies in the rural areas, place them in their own companies and various private companies or public institutes in urban centers such as BRTA. Finally, in chapter nine, I showcased how the deregulation of public education sector in Bangladesh led to the creation of privatized higher education institutes owned either by politicians, or politically affiliated business people, or senior bureaucrats—the rich Bangladeshi capitalists. A similar image can be seen in Bangladesh's privatized banking sector. In each of these examples, due to the patron-client relationship model, the impoverished remain as a subjugated social group. Overall, these evidences indicate that, except for the political and economic elites in Bangladesh, the rest of the social groups have no voice either in the design or deployment of development in the country.

In terms of awareness of the effects of development projects in general, I observed that all my interviewees in rural and urban settings were aware of the fact that Bangladesh has a "bogus democracy" (Chossudovsky 2003) and that the patron-client functional model it follows has given birth to a new economic elite class. However, most of the members of the other social groups—middle-class, intellectuals, professionals, and impoverished—felt their hands were tied. As the stated social groups feel powerless, while some members of each of these social groups leave the country as skilled, semi-skilled workers to developed or semi-developed countries, many find adapting to political party induced corruption more efficient as a survival mechanism, as illustrated in the BRTA case-study in chapter eight.

At the same time, the various social groups of development—professionals, intellectuals, impoverished—felt that they were powerless to influence the existing practices of 'development' because development agency and state generated reports are increasingly being represented through numeric forms. These social groups criticized this practice, recognizing it as a form of enumerative malaise that hides the gap between reality and rhetoric while benefitting the country's economic elites and their allies, which include some economists, development professionals, such as NGO and the World Bank workers, as well as high ranking Bangladeshi government officials. Interestingly, most of the aid agency and state personnel were aware of the local resentment about development, courtesy of dual hegemony, but they continue to not pay attention to that specific social realm.

7.6 Policy Recommendations/Prescriptions

My research goal was not to generate policy recommendations for the Bangladeshi government or the aid development industry. I believe, however, that my research is informative for those organizations and the individuals who work for them, as well as the tax-payers in the developed countries whose tax contributions provide most of the necessary funds to run aid agencies, such as the World Bank and IMF. Additionally, I do not have any illusions about the likelihood of dominant interests within those organizations adopting any of my recommendations. The future achievement of more equality and true democracy will require some shifting of power relations, but that is hard to envision in Bangladesh, given the country's present course of development. While my research is unlikely to solve the interconnected issues and factors that engulf development aid vis-a-vis poverty reduction, the intention of my monograph is to present my findings and concerns to my national and international colleagues and start a discussion based on the following talking points on policy reform.

Given Bangladesh's large and young population base, as outlined in chapter one, I believe we need to learn the reasons for poverty construction from the primary school level. Building upon that, employing critical approaches within the university system could also help the students learn about the capitalist and non-capitalist forms of exploitation that produce poverty. For example, Bangladeshi youth need to learn about their cultural history and how their country is increasingly shaped by broader global economic forces, in addition to economic globalization and poverty. Overall, understanding the reasons and causes behind the construction of poverty could become a gateway to reduce poverty and consequently to the achievement of democracy and liberty in Bangladesh. This could go a long way in return to ensure aid donors properly use development resources to the benefit of the recipients rather than the aid industry as it is manifest in Bangladesh.

As a development alternative, Nobel Laureate, Bangladeshi economist Muhammad Yunus asks the educated and technically savvy young Bangladeshi generation to step up and work within the business sector to develop an alternative development concept or structure that reforms neoliberalism's existing orientations. Muhammad Yunus and Amartya Sen, both of whom are Bengalis, have helped articulate development theories that do not follow the western models and that offer some hope for Bangladesh going forward, if only the country could take a turn towards a more homegrown approach to development. I also agree that alternatives in development can play a far more effective role than the existing Western development industry practices in Bangladesh because the outcomes generated by the former would lead to skilled manpower, as well as better technical, industrial base in Bangladesh. Consequently, these outcomes will help to reduce Bangladesh's existing dependency on foreign imports.

7.7 Limitations and Future Research

Despite the limitations created by my position as an inside/outside observer within the time constraints of a doctoral fieldwork project, I managed to gather a substantive body of data about development aid and poverty in Bangladesh, and about the problematic outcomes of development aid as specifically applied in Bangladesh. More immersive and in-depth fieldwork research is needed, however, to substantiate and expand my critique of the aid industry, specially informed by the voices and experiences of more informants, especially women, to design development projects that mitigate poverty issues in a sustainable manner.

In my own future research projects, I plan to further study the role of Bangladesh's civil society and the military. Given a specific, prioritized set of objectives, there was no room to pursue that in the monograph. However, I acknowledge the importance of the country's civil society and military to the future of the country—in manifesting interests and spirits of citizens, as well as in keeping the democratic elements of a society such as freedom of speech and an independent judiciary. Presently, in the absence of a unified and effective civil society, aid development projects continue in Bangladesh despite their consistent record of failure because they do provide benefits to interest groups—namely employees of the aid industry, bureaucrats, consultants, and corporations in the donor countries. This is why, development aid projects continue to follow the same old path of failure and will continue to do so until transformative change occurs.

I also hope to build on what I have accomplished through my studies by focusing on the issue of emigrant Bangladeshi male and female workers in the Persian Gulf and elsewhere—their employment skills, living conditions, wages, job security, and the circumstances of families they leave behind—wives, children, parents, and siblings. In addition to the legal migrants who generally maintain strong relations with family back home, many migrants work illegally abroad and are unable to return home or have a family. The increase of illegal migration of Bangladeshis to Southern European countries is attributed to the outcomes of poverty and development and in many cases these migrants are now applying for refugee status in their host countries. Migration and refugee experiences have thus become an integral part of Bangladeshi culture and economy in the twenty-first century. Aid projects in support of development and poverty reduction must be informed not only by a better understanding of on-the-ground realities in Bangladesh, but also by a better understanding of the Bangladeshi diasporas scattered throughout the world.

References

Chang, Ha-Joon. 2003. *Kicking Away the Ladder: Development Strategy in Historical Perspective*. London: Anthem Press.

Chossudovsky, Michel. 2003. *The Globalization of Poverty and the New World Order*. Quebec: Global Research.

Escobar, Arturo. 2012 [1995]. *Encountering Development: The Making and Unmaking of the Third World*. Princeton, NJ: Princeton University Press.

Ferguson, James. 1994. *The Anti-Politics Machine: "Development", Depoliticization, and Bureaucratic Power in Lesotho*. Minnesota: University of Minnesota Press.

Frank, Andre Gunder. 1967. *Capitalism and Underdevelopment in Latin America: Historical Studies of Chile and Brazil*. New York: Monthly Review Press.

Gramsci, Antonio. 2010 [1971]. *Selections from the Prison Notebooks*. In Quintin Hoare and Geoffrey Smith (eds.). New York: International Publishers.

Mosse, David. 2005. *Cultivating Development: An Ethnography of Aid Policy and Practice*. London: Pluto Press.

Reinert, Erik. 2007. *How Rich Countries Got Rich and Why Poor Countries Stay Poor*. London: Constable.

Sunkel, Osvaldo. 1972. "Big Business and 'Dependencia'." *Foreign Affairs* 50(April):517–531.

The World Bank. 2018. "Lending - Bangladesh: Commitments by Fiscal Year (in millions of dollars)." Accessed 22 December 2018. http://www.worldbank.org/en/country/Bangladesh/projects.

Urmetzer, Peter. 2003. *From Free Trade to Forced Trade: Canada in the Global Economy*. Toronto: Penguin/McGill Institute.

Bibliography

Ahmad, Ahrar. 2021. "The Politics of Anti-Politics: Corruption, Democracy and the Universities." *The Daily Star*. 8 July. Accessed 22 July 2021. https://www.thedailystar.net/views/opinion/news/the-politics-anti-politics-corruption-democracy-and-the-universities-2124751.

Ahmed, Kamal. 2010. "Bangladesh Army's Advancing Business Interests." Published 15 August 2010. Accessed 21 June 2021. https://www.bbc.com/news/world-south-asia-10801268.

Alam, Shahid M. 2016. *Poverty Rom the Wealth of Nations: Integration and Polarization in the Global Economy Since 1760*. Springer Science and Business Media.

Amundsen, I. 2016. "Democratic Dynasties? Internal Party Democracy in Bangladesh." *Party Politics* 22(1):49–58.

Anderson, Benedict. 1991. *Imagined Communities: Reflections on the Origin and Spread of Nationalism*. London: Verso.

Appadurai, Arjun. 1990. "Disjuncture and Difference in the Global Cultural Economy." *Theory, Culture, and Society* 7(2):295–310.

Apthorpe, Raymond. 2011. "Coda: With Alice in Aidland: A Seriously Satirical Allegory." In David Mosse (ed.), *Adventures in Aidland: The Anthropology of Professionals in International Development*. New York; Oxford: Berghahn Press.

Asian Infrastructure and Investment Bank (AIIB). 2017. Accessed 4 August. https://www.aiib.org/en/index.html.

Atia, M. 2012. "A Way to Paradise: Pious Neoliberalism, Islam, and Faith-Based Development." *Annals of the Association of American Geographers* 102(4):808–827.

M. M. Husain, *Development, Neoliberalism, and Islamism in South Asia*,
https://doi.org/10.1007/978-3-031-03113-7

Atılgan, G. 2012. "Türkiye'de Toplumsal Sınıflar: 1923–2010." In Faruk Alpkaya and Bülent Duru (eds.) *Türkiye'de Toplumsal Yapı ve Değişim*, pp. 323–366. Ankara: Phoenix.

Banerjee, Somaditya. 2018. "Bhadralok Physics and the Making of Modern Science in Colonial India." PhD thesis, University of British Columbia.

Bangladesh Bank. 2016 "Monthly Data of Wage Earner's Remittance." Accessed 24 August 2016. https://www.bb.org.bd/econdata/wageremitance.php.

Bangladesh Road Transport Authority (BRTA). 2014. Last modified 19 March 2014. Accessed 11 September 2014. http://www.brta.gov.bd/index.php/activities.

Bangladesh'r Rajniti. 2021. Accessed 12 May. https://www.facebook.com/Bangladesh.Rajniti/videos/2938393023151233.

Barber, B. R. 1996. *Jihad vs. McWorld: How Globalism and Tribalism Are Reshaping the World*. New York: Ballantine Books.

Beck, Ulrich. 2000. "The Cosmopolitan Perspectives: Sociology of the Second Age of Modernity." *British Journal of Sociology* 51(1):79–105.

Boratav, K. 2014. *Türkiye İktisat Tarihi 1908–2009*. Ankara: İmge.

Brown, W. 2006. "American Nightmare: Neoliberalism, Neoconservatism, and De-Democratization." *Political Theory* 34(6):690–697.

Bullock, Alan, and Trombley, Stephen, eds. (1999). *The New Fontana Dictionary of Modern Thought*. London: HarperCollins.

Calhoun, Carig with Mark Juergensmeyer, and Jonathan Van Antwerpen. 2011. *Rethinking Secularism*. London: Oxford University Press.

Casanova, J. 1994. *Public Religions in the Modern World*. Chicago: University of Chicago Press.

Centre for Policy Dialogue (CPD). 2019. "Education Budget in Bangladesh: An Analysis of Trends, Gaps and Priorities." Accessed 18 March 2019. https://cpd.org.bd/category/policy-briefs/.

Chang, Ha-Joon. 2003. *Kicking Away the Ladder: Development Strategy in Historical Perspective*. London: Anthem Press.

Chatterjee, Partha. 1993. *The Nation and Its Fragments: Colonial and Postcolonial Histories*. Princeton: Princeton University Press.

———. 2004. *The Politics of the Governed*. New York: Columbia University Press.

Chossudovsky, Michel. 2003. *The Globalization of Poverty and the New World Order*. Quebec: Global Research.

Cohn, B. S. 1996. *Colonialism and Its Forms of Knowledge: The British in India*. Princeton: Princeton University Press.

Comaroff, J., and J. Comaroff. 2000. "Millennial Capitalism: First Thoughts on a Second Coming." *Public Culture* 12(2):291–343.

Connolly, W. E. 2005. "The Evangelical-Capitalist Resonance Machine." *Political Theory* 33(6):869–886.

Cooper, Frederick. 2005. *Colonialism in Question: Theory, Knowledge, History*. Berkeley: University of California Press.

Cooper, Frederick, and Randall Packard. 1997. *International Development and the Social Sciences: Essays on the History and Politics of Knowledge*. Berkeley: University of California Press.

Cowen, M. P., and R. W. Shenton 1996. *Doctrines of Development*. London: Routledge.

Deliège, Robert. 2011. "Caste, Class, and Untouchability." In *A Companion to the Anthropology of India*. Singapore: Blackwell.

Dikecx, M. 2006. "Two Decades of French Urban Policy: From Social Development of Neighbourhoods to the Republican Penal State." *Antipode* 38(1):59–81.

Dirks, Nicholas. 2001. *Castes of Mind: Colonialism and the Making of Modern India*. Princeton: Princeton University Press.

Doğan, A. E. 2013. "İslamcı Sermayenin Gelişme Dinamikleri ve 28 Şubat Süreci." In İlhan Uzgel and Bülent Duru (eds.), *AKP Kitabı: Bir Dönüşümün Bilançosu*, pp. 283–306. Ankara: Phoenix.

Easterly, William. 2005. "What Did Structural Adjustment Adjust?: The Association of Policies and Growth with Repeated IMF and World Bank Adjustment Loans." *Journal of Development Economics* 76(1):1–22.

Eaton, Richard M. 1993. *The Rise of Islam and the Bengal Frontier, 1204–1760*. Berkeley: University of California Press.

Eelens, Frank, and J. Speckmann. 1990. "Recruitment of Labour Migrants for the Middle East: The Sri Lankan Case." *International Migration Review* 24(2):297–322.

Edelman, Marc, and Angelique Haugerud. 2005. *The Anthropology of Development and Globalization: From Classical Political Economy to Contemporary Neoliberalism*. Victoria: Blackwell.

El-Sherif, A. 2014. "The Egyptian Muslim Brotherhood's Failures." Published on 1 July 2014. Accessed 6 May 2021. https://carnegieendowment.org/2014/07/01/egyptian-muslim-brotherhood-s-failures-pub-56046.

Elyachar, J. 2005. *Markets of Dispossession: NGOs, Economic Development, and the State in Cairo*. Durham: Duke University Press.

Escobar, Arturo. 1991. "Anthropology and the Development Encounter: The Making and Marketing of Development Anthropology." *American Ethnologist* 18(4):658–682.

———. 2012 [1995]. *Encountering Development: The Making and Unmaking of the Third World*. Princeton, NJ: Princeton University Press.

European Country of Origin Information Network. 2018. "Bangladesh: Freedom of Religion or Belief." Published September 2018. Accessed 12 May 2021. https://www.ecoi.net/en/file/local/1447985/3175_1540665654_2018-09-general-briefings-bangladesh.pdf.

Evans, Mary. 2004. *Killing Thinking: The Death of the Universities*. London: Continuum.

Farmer, Paul. 2003. *Pathologies of Power Health, Human Rights, and the New War on the Poor.* Berkeley and Los Angeles: University of California Press.

Fejerskov, Adrian. 2016. "The Social Construction of Development Cooperation Success and Failure." *Forum for Development Studies* 43(3):365–383.

Feldman, Shelly. 2016. "The Hindu as Other: State, Law, and Land Relations in Contemporary Bangladesh." *South Asia Multidisciplinary Academic Journal* 13(13). https://journals.openedition.org/samaj/4111.

Feldman, Shelly, and Charles Geisler. 2011. "Land Grabbing in Bangladesh: In-Situ Displacement of Peasant Holdings." Paper presented at the International Conference on Global Land Grabbing, University of Sussex, England, 6–8 April 2011.

Ferguson, James. 1994. *The Anti-Politics Machine: "Development", Depoliticization, and Bureaucratic Power in Lesotho.* Minnesota: University of Minnesota Press.

———. 2010. "The Uses of Neoliberalism." *Antipode* 41(s1):166–184.

Financial Express. 2014. "Drivers with Fake Licenses". Posted on 26 January 2014. Accessed 26 October 2014. http://www.thefinancialexpress-bd.com/2014/01/26/15590/index.php.

Frank, Andre Gunder. 1967. *Capitalism and Underdevelopment in Latin America: Historical Studies of Chile and Brazil*. New York: Monthly Review Press.

Friedman, Jonathan. 2007. "Global Systems, Globalization, and Anthropological Theory." In I. Rossi (ed.), *Frontiers of Globalization Research*. Boston, MA: Springer.

Gardner, K., and F. Osella. 2004. "Migration, Modernity and Social Transformation in South Asia: An Introduction." In F. Osella and K. Gardner (eds.) *Migration, Modernity and Social Transformation in South Asia*, pp. xi–xlviii. New Delhi and London: Sage.

Gauthier, F. 2019. "The Marketisation of Religion." In *Religion, Modernity, Globalisation*. London: Routledge.

Gopalakrishnan, S. 2009. *Neoliberalism and Hindutva: Fascism, Free Markets and the Restructuring of Indian Capitalism*. Delhi: Aakar Books.

Gönenç, U. 2019. "Charity State: Neoliberalism, Political Islam, and Class Relations in Turkey." *New Proposals: Journal of Marxism and Interdisciplinary Inquiry* 10(1) April:16–28.

Gramsci, Antonio. 2010 [1971]. *Selections from the Prison Notebooks*. In Quintin Hoare and Geoffrey Smith (eds.). New York: International Publishers.

Griffiths, Martin, and Mubashar Hasan. 2015. "Playing with Fire: Islamism and Politics in Bangladesh." *Asian Journal of Political Science* 23(2):226–241.

Guhathakurta, Meghna, and Willem van Schendel. 2013. *The Bangladesh Reader—History, Culture, Politics*. Durham and London: Duke University Press.

Gupta, Akhil. 1998. *Postcolonial Developments: Agriculture in the Making of Modern India*. Durham: Duke University Press.

Gürel, B. 2015. "Türkiye'de Kırda Sınıf Mücadelelerinin Tarihsel Gelişimi." In Sungur Savran, Kurtar Tanyılmaz, and E. Ahmet Tonak (eds.), *Marksizm ve Sınıflar*, pp. 303–385. Istanbul: Yordam.

Habib, Rafey. 2011. *A History of Literary Criticism: From Plato to the Present*. New York: Wiley-Blackwell.

Harb, M., and L. Deeb. 2011. "Culture as History and Landscape: Hizbullah's Efforts to Shape an Islamic Milieu in Lebanon." *Arab Studies Journal* 19(1):12–45.

Hart, Gillian. 2001. "Development Critiques in the 1990s: Culs de Sacs and Promising Paths." *Progress in Human Geography* 25(4):649–658.

Harvey, David. 2005. *A Brief History of Neo-Liberalism*. Oxford: Oxford University Press.

Hashim, A. 1965. *As I See It*. Dacca: Islamic Academy.

Hegel, G. W. F. 1979 [1807]. *Phenomenology of Spirit*. Oxford: Oxford University Press.

Hossen, Anwar. 2014. "Water Policy and Governance for the Empowerment of River Basin Communities in Rural Bangladesh." PhD thesis, University of British Columbia Okanagan.

Hoşgör, E. 2015. "Islamic Capital." In Neşecan Balkan, Erol Balkan, and Ahmet Öncü (eds.), *The Neoliberal Landscape and the Rise of Islamist Capital in Turkey*, pp. 142–165. New York: Berghahn Books.

Hudelson, Richard. 1999. *Modern Political Philosophy*. New York: M.E. Sharpe, 1999.

Huntington, Samuel P. 2005. *Soldier and the State: The Theory and Politics of Civil–Military Relations*. Cambridge, MA: Belknap Press.

Huq, Samia. 2013. "Defining Self and Other: Bangladesh's Secular Aspirations and Its Writing of Islam." *Economic and Political Weekly* 48(50):51–61.

Husain, Matt. 2017. "Aid-Effectiveness: On the Radar and Off the Radar." *Development Policy Review* 35(3):337–348.

Husain, Matt Mustahid. 2019. "Who Reaps the Benefit?—Dual Hegemony and the Politics of Development in Bangladesh." PhD thesis, University of British Columbia.

Husain, Matt, and Karina Osswald. 2016. "Zombie Graduates Driven by Rickshaw Faculty—A Qualitative Case Study: Private Universities in Urban Bangladesh." *Policy Futures in Education* 14(7):1020–1035.

Husain, Matt, and Sebastian Kolesar. 2018. "Can Technology Change the Existing Culture?—A Case-Study on Bangladeshi Public Sector." *Development in Practice* 28(1):152–164.

IFAD Group. 2021. "Management." Accessed 21 July. http://www.ifadmultiproducts.com/about/.

International Development Association (IDA). 2018. "FY18 Top 10 Borrowers." Accessed 17 September 28, 2018. http://ida.worldbank.org/financing/ida-financing.

Islam, Nazrul. 2017. "Middle-Class in Bangladesh." *Bangladesh e-Journal of Sociology* 14(1) January:4–15. Accessed 27 August 2018. http://www.bangladeshsociology.org/BEJS14.1.pdf.

Jahan, Afrose Chaity. 2018. "Budget Allocations for Health, Education Continue to Shrink." *Dhaka Tribune*. Accessed 18 March 2019. https://www.dhakatribune.com/bangladesh/2018/06/29/budget-allocations-for-health-education-continue-to-shrink.

Janowitz, Morris. 1988. *Military Institutions and Coercion in Developing Nations: The Military in the Political Development of New Nations*. Chicago: University of Chicago Press.

Joya, A. 2020. *The Roots of Revolt: A Political Economy of Egypt from Nasser to Mubarak*. Cambridge: Cambridge University Press.

Kabeer, Naila. 2008. *Mainstreaming Gender and Social Protection in the Informal Economy*. London: Commonwealth Secretariat.

———. 2011. "The Quest for National Identity: Women, Islam and the State in Bangladesh." In Kamala Visweswaran (ed.), *Perspectives on Modern South Asia: A Reader in Culture, History, and Representation*, pp. 139–153. Malden: Wiley-Blackwell.

Kabir, Ariful Haq. 2010. "Neo-Liberal Policy in the Higher Education Sector in Bangladesh: Autonomy of Public Universities and the Role of the State." *Policy Futures in Education* 8(6):619–630.

Kabir, Bhuian. 2006. *Politics and Development of the Jamaat-e-Islami Bangladesh*. New Delhi: South Asian Publishers.

Kabir, Shahriar. 2007. *Cultural History of Secular Humanism in Bangladesh*. Dhaka: Dana Printers Limited.

Karaman, O. 2013. "Urban Neoliberalism with Islamic Characteristics." *Urban Studies* (Edinburgh, Scotland) 50(16):3412–3427.

Katz, Cindi. 2001. "Vagabond Capitalism and the Necessity of Social Reproduction." *Antipode* 33(4):709–728.

Karim, Lamia. 2008. "Demystifying Micro-Credit: The Grameen Bank, NGOs, and Neoliberalism in Bangladesh." *Cultural Dynamics* 20(5):5–30.

Keynes, John Maynard. 1936. *The General Theory of Employment, Interest and Money*. London: Palgrave Macmillan.

Khan, H. M. 2019. "The Changing Face of Political Islam in Bangladesh: From Compromise to Confrontation? (1991–2016)." *Journal of Bangladesh Studies* 21(2):45–59.

Khandker, Shahidur. 2005. *Microfinance and Poverty: Evidence Using Panel Data from Bangladesh*. Published by Oxford University Press on behalf of the World Bank.

Khilnani, Sunil. 1997. *The Idea of India*. London: Penguin UK.

Kibria, Nazli. 2008. "Muslim Encounters in the Global Economy Identity Developments of Labor Migrants from Bangladesh to the Middle East." *Ethnicities* 8(4):518–535; 097077. https://doi.org/10.1177/1468796808097077.

———. 2011. "Working Hard for the Money: Bangladesh Faces Challenges of Large-Scale Labour Migration." *Migration Policy Institute*. Modified 9 August. Accessed 9 September 2015. http://www.migrationpolicy.org/article/working-hard-money-bangladesh-faces-challenges-large-scale-labor-migration.

Kissinger, H. 1994. *Diplomacy*. New York: Simon and Schuster.

Klytchnikova, Irina, and Ndiame Diop. 2006. "Trade Reforms, Farm Productivity, and Poverty in Bangladesh." *Policy Research Working Paper Series*, No. 3980. World Bank, Washington, DC.

Laurie, Timothy. 2015. "Masculinity Studies and the Jargon of Strategy: Hegemony, Tautology, Sense." *Journal of the Theoretical Humanities* 20(1):13–30.

Leftwich, Adrian. 2005. "Politics in Command: Development Studies and the Rediscovery of Social Science." *New Political Economy* 10(4):573–607.

Leys, Colin. 1996. *The Rise and Fall of Development Theory*. Oxford: Oxford Press.

Lewis, D. 2011. *Bangladesh: Politics, Economy and Civil Society*. Cambridge: Cambridge University Press.

Mahmood, Muhammad. 2017. "Income Inequality and Poverty in Bangladesh." *The Financial Express*. 25 June. https://thefinancialexpress.com.bd/views/income-inequality-and-poverty-in-bangladesh-1510415084.

Mahmud, Faisal. 2018. "Bangladesh to Join Space Age Amid Skepticism About Costs." *Nikkei Asian Review*. Accessed 22 December 2018. https://asia.nikkei.com/Economy/Bangladesh-to-join-space-age-amid-skepticism-about-costs.

Masud, T. 2010. "Runway." *Bangla Movie*. Accessed 4 September 2015. https://youtu.be/cVHr6tMpU_I.

Max-Neef, M. 2012. "Keynote at Zermatt Summit." Accessed 1 July 2020. https://www.youtube.com/watch?v=5EURJI9x9Qs.

Mishra, Pankaj. 2013. *From the Ruins of Empire: The Revolt Against the West and the Remaking of Asia*. Toronto: Doubleday.

Morris-Jones, W. H. 1964. *The Government and Politics of India*. London: Hutchinson University Library.

Mosse, David. 2005. *Cultivating Development: An Ethnography of Aid Policy and Practice*. London: Pluto Press.

———. 2010. "A Relational Approach to Durable Poverty, Inequality and Power." *Journal of Development Studies* 46(7):1156–1178.

Mosse, David, and David Lewis (eds.). 2005. *The Aid Effect: Giving and Governing in International Development*. London: Pluto Press.

Naidoo, Rajani, and Ian Jamieson. 2005. "Empowering Participants or Corroding Learning? Towards a Research Agenda on the Impact of Student Consumerism in Higher Education." *Journal of Education Policy* 20(3):267–281.

Nurunnabi, Mohammad. 2018. "Accounting for Accountability: A Critical Reflection on the Private Higher Education in Bangladesh." *Administration and Society* 50(3):429–470.

Nuruzzaman, Mohammed. 2004. "Neo-Liberal Economic Reforms, the Rich and the Poor in Bangladesh." *Journal of Contemporary Asia* 34(1):33–54.

OXFAM. 2017. *An Economy for the 99%.* Canada: Oxfam. Accessed 20 January 2018. https://www.oxfam.ca/sites/default/files/file_attachments/bp-economy-for-99percent-160117-summ-embargo-en.pdf.

———. 2019. "Billionaire Fortunes Grew by $2.5 Billion a Day Last Year as Poorest Saw Their Wealth Fall." Accessed 22 January 2019. https://www.oxfam.org/en/pressroom/pressreleases/2019-01-18/billionaire-fortunes-grew-25-billion-day-last-year-poorest-saw.

Öztürk, Ö. 2011. "Türkiye Finans Kapitalinin Dışa Açılması." *Devrimci Marksizm* 13–14:106–132.

Palley, Thomas. 2005. "From Keynesianism to Neoliberalism: Shifting Paradigms." In *Neoliberalism—A Critical Reader*. London: Pluto Press.

Parry, Jonathan P. 2000. "'The Crisis of Corruption' and the 'The Idea of India': A Worm's Eye View." In I. Pardo (ed.), *The Morals of Legitimacy*, pp. 27–55. New York and Oxford: Berghahn Books.

Paul, S., and Shah, M. 1997. "Corruption in Public Service Delivery." In S. Guhan and S. Paul (eds.), *Corruption in India: Agenda for Action*, pp. 144–163. New Delhi: Vision Books.

Peck, Jamie. 2008. "Remaking Laissez Faire." *Progress in Human Geography* 32(1):3–43.

———. 2010. *Constructions of Neoliberal Reason*. Oxford: Oxford University Press.

Peek, L. 2005. "Becoming Muslim: The Development of a Religious Identity." *Sociology of Religion* 66(3):215–242.

Percy, Alisa. 2011. "A New Age in Higher Education or Just a Little Bit of History Repeating?: Linking the Past, Present and Future of All in Australia." *Journal of Academic Language and Learning* 5(2):131–144.

Perlmutter, Amos, and Valerie Plave Bennett (eds.). 1980. *The Political Influence of the Military*. New Haven: Yale University Press.

Polanyi, Karl. 2008 [1944]. *The Great Transformation: The Political and Economic Origins of Our Time*. Boston: Beacon Press.

Prime Bank. 2014. "Education Loan." Modified 30 May 2011. Accessed 7 May 2014. https://www.primebank.com.bd/index.php/home/education_loan.

Quadir, Fahim. 2015. *Civil Society in Asia: In Search of Democracy and Development in Bangladesh*. Aldershot: Ashgate.

Quddus, Munir, and Salim Rashid. 2000. "The Worldwide Movement in Private Universities: Revolutionary Growth in Post-Secondary Higher Education." *American Journal of Economics and Sociology* 59(3):487–516.

Qutb, S. 2006 [1964]. *Milestones*. The Mother Mosque Foundation. Cedar Rapids, IA.

Rahim, Aminur. 2007. "Communalism and Nationalism in Bangladesh." *Journal of Asian and African Studies* 42(6):551–572.

Rahman, Mizanur Md. 2012. "Bangladeshi Labour Migration to the Gulf States: Patterns of Recruitment and Processes." *Canadian Journal of Development Studies* 33(2):214–230.

Rankin, Katharine. 2001. "Governing Development: Neoliberalism, Microcredit, and Rational Economic Woman." *Economy and Society* 30(1):18–37.

Ratha, Dilip, and William Shaw. 2012. "South-South Migration and Remittances." *Migration Policy Institute*. Accessed 9 September 2015. http://www.migrationpolicy.org/article/south-south-migration-and-remittances.

Reinert, Erik. 2007. *How Rich Countries Got Rich and Why Poor Countries Stay Poor*. London: Constable.

Reuters. 2007. "Bangladesh's Nobel Winner Names New Political Party." Accessed 14 March 2019. https://www.reuters.com/article/us-bangladesh-yunus/bangladesh-nobel-winner-names-new-political-party-idUSDHA33014220070218.

Riaz, Ali. 2004. *God Willing: The Politics of Islamism in Bangladesh*. Oxford: Rawman and Littlefield.

———. 2012. *Inconvenient Truths About Bangladeshi Politics*. Bangladesh: Prothoma Prokashan.

———. 2014. *Culture of Fear: The Political Economy of Terror and Violence in Bangladesh* (in Bangla). Dhaka: Prothoma Prokashan.

Riaz, Ali, and Jessica Bastian. 2011. "Islamist Militancy in Bangladesh: Regional and Extra-Regional Dimensions." In Ali Riaz and C. Fair (eds.), *Political Islam and Governance in Bangladesh*. London: Routledge.

Riddell, Roger. 2014. *Does Foreign Aid Really Work?* New York: Oxford University Press.

Ritzer, George. 1998. *The McDonaldization Thesis*. London: Sage.

Rosenblum, N. 2003. "Religious Parties, Religious Political Identity, and the Cold Shoulder of Liberal Democratic Thought." *Ethical Theory and Moral Practice* 6(1):23–53.

Roy, A. 2014 [1983]. *The Islamic Syncretistic Tradition in Bengal*. Princeton: Princeton University Press.

Rudnyckyj, D. 2009. "Spiritual Economies: Islam and Neoliberalism in Contemporary Indonesia." *Cultural Anthropology* 24(1), February:104–141.

Ruud, A. E. 2011. "Democracy in Bangladesh: A Village View." In S. Toft Madsen, K. B. Nielsen, and U. Skoda (eds.), *Trysts with Democracy: Political Practice in South Asia*. London and New York: Anthem Press.

Saad-Filho, A. 2003. "Introduction." In Alfredo Saad Filho (ed.), *AntiCapitalism: A Marxist Introduction*, pp. 1–26. London: Pluto.

Santos, Theotonio Dos. 1971. "The Structure of Dependence." *American Economic Review* 60(May 1970):231–236.

Schenoni, Luis. 2018. "The Southern African Unipolarity." *Journal of Contemporary African Studies* 36(2):207–228.

Schiff, Rebecca. 2009. "Concordance and Culture from the Military–Industrial Complex to Corporate Philanthropy." In *The Military and Domestic Politics: A Concordance Theory of Civil-Military Relations*. London; New York: Routledge.

Schmidt, G. 2004. "Islamic Identity Formation Among Young Muslims: The Case of Denmark, Sweden and the US." *Journal of Muslim Minority Affairs* 24(1):31–45.

Sen, Amartya. 1982. *Poverty and Famines*. New York: Norton.

———. 2000. *Development as Freedom*. New York: Anchor Books.

———. 2006. *Identity of Violence: The Illusion of Destiny*. Oxford: Oxford University Press.

Sen, Binayak. 2003. "Drivers of Escape and Descent: Changing Household Fortunes in Rural Bangladesh." *World Development* 31(3):513–534.

Sena Kalyan Shongstha (SKS). 2022. https://www.senakalyan.org/corporate-overview.php.

Shendel, V. W. 2009. *A History of Bangladesh*. Cambridge: Cambridge University Press.

Siddiqa, Ayesha. 2011. "The Evolution of Civil–Military Relations in South Asia." In E. Sridharan (ed.), *International Relations Theory and South Asia: Security, Political Economy, Domestic Politics, Identities, and Images*, vol. 1. Oxford: Oxford University Press. https://doi.org/10.1093/acprof:oso/9780198069652.001.0001.

Siddiqi, Dina. 2018. "Secular Quests, National Others: Revisiting Bangladesh's Constituent Assembly Debates." *Asian Affairs* 49:1–21.

______. 2019. "Exceptional Sexuality in a Time of Terror: "Muslim" Subjects and Dissenting/Unmournable Bodies." *South Asia Multidisciplinary Academic Journal* 20(20):online. https://doi.org/10.4000/samaj.5069.

Skinner, Andrew. 1999. *The Glasgow Edition of the Works and Correspondence of Adam Smith.* Oxford: Clarendon Press.

Sobhan, Rehman. 1984. *The Crisis of External Dependence: The Political Economy of Foreign Aid to Bangladesh.* London, UK; Bangladesh: Zed Press University Press.

Statistics Portal. 2018. "Population Density of Bangladesh from 2005 to 2016 (in People Per Square Kilometer)." Accessed 8 October 2018. https://www.statista.com/statistics/778381/bangladesh-population-density/.

Stepan, Alfred. 1971. *The Military in Politics Changing Patterns in Brazil.* Princeton, NJ: Princeton University Press.

Stiglitz, Joseph. 2008. "Is There a Post-Washington Consensus Consensus?" In N. Serra and J. Stiglitz (eds.), *The Washington Consensus Reconsidered: Towards a New Global Governance.* Oxford: Oxford University Press.

Stille, M. 2020. *Islamic Sermons and Public Piety in Bangladesh—The Poetics of Popular Preaching.* London: Bloomsbury Publishing.

Sunandapriya, B. V. 2013. *Attacks on Buddhists: Ominous Inaction.* Dhaka: Sougata Prakashan.

Sunkel, Osvaldo. 1972. "Big Business and 'Dependencia'." *Foreign Affairs* 50(April):517–531.

Tasnim, Farhat. 2007. "Civil Society in Bangladesh: Vibrant but Not Vigilant." PhD Dissertation. Department of Political Science, University of Tsukuba, Japan. Accessed 17 September 2014. http://www.tulips.tsukuba.ac.jp/limedio/dlam/B27/B2782934/1.pdf.

Tasnim, Eshita. 2012. "The Minority Protection." *The Daily Star.* 20 October. Accessed 12 August 2016.

Tharoor, Shashi. 2015. *India Shastra: Reflections on the Nation in Our Time.* Delhi: Aleph Book Company.

The Daily Star. 2010. "Amended Law on Private Universities Okayed." Accessed 4 January 2015. http://www.thedailystar.net/newDesign/news-details.php?nid=123568.

———. 2019. "Role of Foreign Aid in Bangladesh." Accessed 4 July 2019. https://www.thedailystar.net/business/role-foreign-aid-bangladesh-1603780.

The Economist. 2021. "Bangladesh's Government Lavishes Money on the Army". Published 1 February 2021. Accessed 12 February 2022. https://www.economist.com/asia/2021/02/11/bangladeshs-government-lavishes-money-on-the-army.

The Independent. 2017. "Private Universities—Only 12 Out of 51 Move to Permanent Campuses." Published 19 January. Accessed 9 August 2017. http://www.theindependentbd.com/arcprint/details/77136/2017-01-19.

The World Bank. 2015. "Bangladesh Projects & Programs." Accessed 9 January 2015. http://www.worldbank.org/en/country/bangladesh/projects.

———. 2016. "Migration and Remittances Recent Developments and Outlook." *Migration and Development Brief* 26. Accessed 1 September 2016. http://pubdocs.worldbank.org/en/661301460400427908/MigrationandDevelopmentBrief26.pdf.

———. 2017a. "How Do We Classify Countries?" Accessed 11 June. https://blogs.worldbank.org/opendata/new-country-classifications-income-level-2017-2018.

———. 2017b. "Bangladesh." Accessed 27 April. http://data.worldbank.org/country/bangladesh.

———. 2018a. "International Debt Statistics." Accessed 12 June. https://www.indexmundi.com/facts/bangladesh/ibrd-loans-and-ida-credits.

———. 2018b. "Climate Change: Overview." Accessed 2 October 2018. http://www.worldbank.org/en/topic/climatechange/overview.

———. 2019a. "Government Expenditure on Education, Total (% of GDP)." United Nations Educational, Scientific, and Cultural Organization (UNESCO) Institute for Statistics. Accessed 18 March 2019. https://data.worldbank.org/indicator/SE.XPD.TOTL.GD.ZS?end=2018&start=2012.

———. 2019b. "Poverty Overview." Accessed 29 June 2019. https://www.worldbank.org/en/topic/poverty/overview.

de Tocqueville, Alexis. 1901 [1835]. *Democracy in America*. London: Saunders and Otley.

Turner, B. S. 2011. *Religion and Modern Society—Citizenship, Secularisation and the State*. Cambridge: Cambridge University Press.

Uddin, Sufia M. 2006. *Constructing Bangladesh: Religion, Ethnicity and Language in an Islamic Nation*. Chapel Hill, NC: University of North Carolina Press.

United Nations (UN). 2015. "Report of the Special Rapporteur on Freedom of Religion or Belief on His Visit to Bangladesh." 9 September 2015. Accessed 5 August 2016. http://www.ohchr.org/Documents/Issues/Religion/A-HRC-31-18-Add2.pdf.

———. 2016. "Charter of the United Nations." Accessed 5 November 2016. http://www.un.org/en/documents/charter/.

University Grants Commission of Bangladesh. 2015. "List of Private Universities." Accessed 9 August 2015. http://www.ugc.gov.bd/university/?action=private.

Urmetzer, Peter. 2003. *From Free Trade to Forced Trade: Canada in the Global Economy*. Toronto: Penguin/McGill Institute.

USAID. 2016. "Mission, Vision and Values." Accessed 12 November. https://www.usaid.gov/who-we-are/mission-vision-values.

Venugopal, Rajesh. 2015. "Neoliberalism as Concept." *Economy and Society* 44(2):165–187.

Wallerstein, Immanuel. 1974. *The Capitalist World Economy: Essays*. New York: Cambridge University Press.

———. 1976. "Semi-Peripheral Countries and the Contemporary World Crisis." *Theory and Society* 3:462–463.

———. 2010. "Northeast Asia in the Multipolar World System." *Asian Perspective* 34(4):191–205.

White, J. 2002. *Islamist Mobilization in Turkey: A Study in Vernacular Politics*. Seattle: University of Washington Press.

Wilken, Rowan, and Christian McCrea. 2013. "The Living Dead and the Dead Living: Contagion and Complicity in Contemporary Universities." In *Zombies in The Academy: Living Death in Higher Education*. Chicago: University of Chicago Press.

World Ultra Wealth Report. 2018. "Rich in Bangladesh Rising Faster Than Anywhere." Accessed 9 October 2018. https://www.thedailystar.net/online/news/fastest-growing-rich-population-country-bangladesh-report-1632385.

World Watch Monitor. 2015. *Attack on Nuns Said to Be First Ever in Bangladesh*. Published 12 August. Accessed 12 May 2021. https://www.worldwatchmonitor.org/2014/08/attack-on-nuns-said-to-be-first-ever-in-bangladesh/.

Yapa, Lakshman. 1996. "What Causes Poverty? A Postmodern View." *Annals of the Association of American Geographers* 86(4):707–728.

Yunus, Muhammad. 2010. *Building Social Business: The New Kind of Capitalism that Serves Humanity's Most Pressing Needs*. Dhaka: University Press Limited.

———. 2012. "Insight: Ideas for Change—Social Business—Muhammad Yunus." Accessed 25 January 2019. https://www.youtube.com/watch?v=5Q2T7TEy9tE&t=4s.

Zaman, Hassan, with Ambar Narayan, and Aphichoke Kotikula. 2010. "Are Bangladesh's Recent Gains in Poverty Reduction Different from the Past?" *Bangladesh Development Studies* XXXV(1):1–26.

Zaman, Tahir. 2014. "Political Islam in Neoliberal Times." *OpenDemocracy*. 17 November 2014. Accessed 5 May 2021. https://www.opendemocracy.net/en/north-africa-west-asia/political-islam-in-neoliberal-times/.

Index

M. M. Husain, *Development, Neoliberalism, and Islamism in South Asia*, https://doi.org/10.1007/978-3-031-03113-7

The manufacturer's authorised representative in the EU is Springer Nature Customer Service Centre GmbH, Europaplatz 3, 69115 Heidelberg, Germany. If you have any concerns regarding our products, please contact ProductSafety@springernature.com

Printed and bound by CPI Group (UK) Ltd, Croydon, CR0 4YY
22/09/2026
02220991-0017